Judi James is a leading television expert in body language, social behaviour, image, workplace culture and communication skills and has her own Channel Five series, *Naked Celebrity*. Judi also appears regularly on *Big Brother on the Couch*, *The Paul O'Grady Show*, *The Xtra Factor*, *Newsnight* and *Sky News*.

Judi started her career as a leading catwalk model and trained many big names at her modelling school in Chelsea, including Naomi Campbell. She has had six novels published, including the bestseller *Supermodel*, and has written ten non-fiction books. Judi also writes regular weekly columns for *You* magazine and has a celebrity problem page in *Zest*.

'We need someone like Judi to slash through the spin and show us what the stars really mean' *Daily Mail*

'Top image consultant and body language guru' *Elle*

'Britain's top body language expert' *Sunday People*

D1350689

To my mother, Renee Sale

THE BODY LANGUAGE BIBLE

The hidden meaning behind people's gestures and expressions

Judi James

Vermilion
LONDON

5 7 9 10 8 6 4

Published in 2008 by Vermilion, an imprint of Ebury Publishing

A Random House Group Company

The Random House Group Limited Reg. No. 954009

Addresses for companies within the Random House Group
can be found at www.rbooks.co.uk

A CIP catalogue record for this book is available from the British Library

The Random House Group Limited supports The Forest Stewardship Council (FSC),
the leading international forest certification organisation. All our titles that are printed
on Greenpeace-approved FSC-certified paper carry the FSC logo. Our paper procurement
policy can be found at www.rbooks.co.uk/environment

Mixed Sources
Product group from well-managed
forests and other controlled sources
www.fsc.org   Cert no. TT-COC-2139
© 1996 Forest Stewardship Council

Printed and bound in Great Britain by
CPI Cox & Wyman, Reading, RG1 8EX

ISBN 9780091922115

Copies are available at special rates for bulk orders. Contact the sales
development team on 020 7840 8487 for more information.

To buy books by your favourite authors and register for offers, visit www.rbooks.co.uk

The information in this book has been compiled by way of general guidance
in relation to the specific subject of body language. It is not a substitute and should not
be relied on for professional advice. So far as the author is aware the information given is
up to date as at March 2008. Practice, laws and regulations change, however, and the
reader should obtain up to date professional advice on any such issues. The author and
publishers disclaim, as far as the laws allow, any liability arising directly or indirectly
from the use or misuse of the information contained in this book.

CONTENTS

INTRODUCTION

Body language is the most fluent, lyrical, revealing and significant form of communication. As an off-shoot of the psychology of human behaviour it is intriguing, exciting, fascinating and fun – and yet ultimately frustrating. As a communication skill your body language accounts for over 50 per cent of the perceived impact of all your face-to-face messages and so you underestimate its power and influence at your peril. By creating and defining your own body language and therefore your own image you will avoid allowing others to perceive you in a way that will have more to do with assumption and misunderstanding than real skills and abilities. However body language is also a much mis-understood subject and a lot of the current advice on the subject is drivel. By using terms like body language 'tells' and analysing gestures in a simplistic, comic-book style along the lines of 'scratching your nose means you're lying', many psychologists, TV magicians and experts have done a lot to mislead the public, therefore damaging what should be primarily an instinctive, sometimes random but nevertheless revealing process.

Do you believe that crossing your arms means you're defen-sive? Or that someone stroking their hair must be flirting with

1

you? Then you've been reading the wrong books, because the fact is that body language is not a precise science. Tempting though it is to claim otherwise, any one gesture can be interpreted in several different ways, just as words can have several meanings. Crossing your arms could mean you feel anxious or angry – or simply that the room's too cold. Arm-folding can be performed to signal displeasure or cut-off but it is also what's called a discovered action, something we do just because it feels comfortable. Nose-touching could show you're covering your mouth to conceal a lie, but it could just as easily mean you've got an itchy nose. Some gestures are inborn, meaning you do them out of instinct and have very little control over them.

To understand words we have to place them into the context of a sentence, and it's just the same with body language gestures, except the sentence is formed by all your other movements and signals. This is why I wrote this book. When I'm training or speaking at conferences one of the most frequently asked questions is what one gesture or another means, as though my studies and experience have endowed me with an almost mystical ability to read people's minds by a single movement or roll of the eyes. Easy and tempting though it would be to go along with this misconception, I have to admit that it's just not that simple. So here are the facts:

- Your own body language signals release thousands of subtle and subconscious signals about you as you speak.
- Your signals can be responsible for success or failure at any stage of your career, social or sex life.
- You are probably unaware of most of your signals.
- Your body language messages are seen by others as a more honest and reliable expression of your thoughts and

feelings than your words. When your words are at odds with your gestures it's your gestures that will be seen as the truth.

- By learning about your own signals and then working to improve them you will enhance your effect and image.

- By studying others' body language signals and increasing your visual perceptions you will find it easier to understand the emotions and thoughts behind their words.

- Look for 'clues' or what are called cues, not 'tells'. This means taking each movement and gesture and then evaluating it in the context of other movements, not isolating them in a 'one size fits all' way.

- By reading other people you will enhance your understanding of them, getting 100 per cent more value out of all your face-to-face communications.

- The good news is that we're *all* experts on body language. You read it all the time and you have done since you were 15 minutes old. By spending some time studying or even rediscovering this very basic of human skills you'll be tapping into what was always intended to be an essential part of our social evolution.

I spend a vast part of my career making body language more accessible and even fun, and I love applying it to politicians, royals, celebrities and – of course – *Big Brother* housemates. All these characters place huge emphasis on selling the 'right' image to the public and it's educational – and good fun – to probe and analyse to discover what might really be going on behind the scenes.

However, making a subject accessible shouldn't mean it gets diluted into a few misleading 'facts' and 'truisms' that risk damaging, rather than enhancing, a super-effective communication process.

By seeing body language in a one-dimensional way we risk placing it in the same category as pseudo-scientific and ultimately unsubstantiated theories such as astrology. Unlike astrology, though, I can prove to you that body language works. How? Look at any other animal. Humans are the only animals to communicate through the medium of words. The rest of the animal kingdom manages very well on what are primarily non-verbal signals. I recently spent several hours watching apes communicating with one another; I saw how the efficiency of their communication linked directly to their survival. Watching a female ape bonding with an abandoned baby ape via submission signals, stage-by-stage touch and some periods of complete back-off reminded me just how much we lost when we learnt to talk. Words might have made human communication easier but they have also made it much harder for us to understand one another, especially where emotions are concerned. And yet many of the ape gestures still have their counterparts in your 'human ape' communications.

Your Image and Personal Marketing Processes

Your image is important – probably even more important than you realise – and your body language is a vital component in creating that image and therefore selling yourself. We exist in an image-conscious and image-compliant society where looking the best wins hands down over being the best. Is this fair? Probably not, but it's still a fact of life. As the Internet, texts and emails have created a vast, unmanageable silo of dead communication so we've come to realise that we're increasingly reliant on visual signals and cues to deliver the real story behind all the spin and hype. This rabid distrust and need for endorsement or proof of honesty is a syndrome I've identified as 'show, don't tell'. In any key situation, from recruitment selection to picking a prime minister, we're increasingly drawn towards using the evidence of our eyes over that of our ears. Ideally the 'show' should come from deeds rather than body image, but another symptom of modern life is that we live in what's called the cult of competitive busy-ness. Put bluntly, we don't have enough hours in the day to make measured decisions about people or their talents based on what they do or what they've done in the past.

Big Business

The image you project is especially vital to your job. Do you ever feel invisible or see your voice, ideas and potential getting lost because your communications fail to meet their target audience? Communication frustration is a common business disease, which is why using your body language as a tool to get ahead is more important than ever before. When no one is listening to your words why not let your body do the talking for you?

We always hear that size isn't important, yet when it comes to modern business it's nevertheless king. Companies rate size as a measure of success and are therefore expanding like never before. When I train managers I'm often asked how they can spot signs of stress or conflict in their teams. The problem they have is that their teams are so large they rarely get to see them, except when they have time to walk the job or when they have a crisis meeting like a disciplinary.

To get on in big business then, you have to first get the attention of the people who count and then present yourself positively and as quickly as possible, often in short sharp bites. For many workers this has led to an ongoing sales-pitch culture with the article on sale being the worker themself. Self-marketing is currently a popular corporate subject while 'keeping your head down and doing your job well' is not.

Gut Reactions

How often do you hear people relying on 'gut reaction' to make important decisions about other people? Sounds random? Many psychologists argue that your 'gut reactions' are really decisions based on the assimilations of a whole raft of complex visual information that you have read subconsciously. Even people pitching for the top jobs have to be aware of it.

Gordon Brown's first keynote pitch for the role of prime minister came a few days after Tony Blair announced the date he'd be stepping down. Brown was at great pains to emphasise that he wouldn't be a celebrity politician concerned with spin and image. Yet as he spoke it was obvious to anyone that he was sporting a new hairdo, a whiter-looking smile and a suspiciously well-cut suit. The core story in the press the next day centred around the fact that his autocue was positioned in a way to obscure his face. He still moved into No. 10 but I bet those are errors he won't be making again!

Your image counts, then, probably more than ever before. Get it wrong and your hidden talents could go unrecognised and unrewarded. Get your image right, though, and you'll increase your status, pulling power and promotion prospects.

But *The Body Language Bible* isn't just about *your* image alone. Much of the book is devoted to the skill of understanding others. By studying the psychology of your own communication you'll also obtain a clearer understanding of the ways that people around you transmit and receive non-verbal messages, learning to read between the lines of everyday communication, giving you a clear psychological advantage in any situation.

PART ONE: BODY LANGUAGE BASICS

This first part of *The Body Language Bible* will take you through the psychology of bodytalk, enabling you to understand the how and why of all those non-verbal signals.

In these chapters you'll learn fascinating facts about animal signals that link us with our evolutionary ancestors much more closely than you probably realise. Did you know that flirting at work is all about status submission and keeping the peace in the office? Or that shaking a client by the hand and smiling to create rapport are both gestures evolved from ape behaviour? Did you ever wonder why, when you get agitated by a colleague or boss at a business meeting, you end up chewing your pen or dismantling a paperclip? All these things and more will be explained here.

The information in this part of the book will help you understand the processes of communication in a way that will enable you to be far more effective at reading and transmitting high-impact signals. You'll gain a unique insight into the instinctive methods both animals and the human animal use and how and why we read other humans in the same time it takes to blink an eye.

1

HOW IT'S DONE

It's hard to define 'perfect' body language but of course I'm going to because that's what I'm here for. I aim to help and I aim to please! Here's your first killer fact, which is all about the breakdown of the perceived effect of your three forms of communication. It's one of the most important facts in this book, so get it tattooed on your body somewhere lest you forget:

In face-to-face communication your words account for as little as 7 per cent of the perceived impact of the communication. Your vocal tone is about 38 per cent but your non-verbal signals take the lion's share with around 55 per cent.

Perceived impact of your message
Words: 7%
Tone of voice: 38%
Non-verbal: 55%

Your second killer fact: how you use these three forms of communication can make all the difference between successful communications that have meaning and effect and the type that nobody believes or notices. Congruence is key.

A BRIEF GUIDE TO CONGRUENCE

This is the perfect communication, meaning your words, tone and non-verbal gestures are all dancing to the same rumba. They give out a matching message and they complement one another. This means you'll look honest, genuine, as though you really mean what you're saying. Congruent bodytalk is going to be your goal throughout this book.

It's vital that your communications look congruent. You'd think this would be easy enough when you genuinely *do* mean what you say, but it's not. Incongruent communication doesn't just happen when you're lying or trying to mask or deceive. Your body language signals can go skidding out of kilter for several reasons. The most common one is shyness or embarrassment. Shyness produces physical awkwardness. The more you feel you're being watched or scrutinised the more awkward your body language becomes, so by the time you try to speak it's unlikely you'll manage to produce a full set of signals. You could tell a client you're pleased to see them and this could well be true, but if shyness makes your eyes flick to the floor as you say it, or your handshake is weak, or you fold your arms into a protective barrier, it's unlikely they will believe what you've just told them.

Tips on How to Look Congruent

- **Focus on your goals before you speak.**

  This will motivate you, making your words feel real, which should make your gestures feel genuine, rather than coming across as rehearsed.

- **Sell your message to yourself first.**

  If you believe what you're saying your body will fall into synchronisation.

- **Avoid exaggerations when you're trying to be convincing.**
  The more you stress your point the more chance your gestures will let you down.

- **Control your breathing and de-stress your body before you speak.**
  When pressure builds up your muscles tense, making natural-looking body language impossible. Breathe out slowly to relax your body and give your hands and feet a little shake to relax the muscles in your arms and legs.

- **If your shoulder muscles are tense your entire body will look awkward.**
  Drop them back and down and stretch your neck upward as this will unlock your posture.

- **Genuine gestures precede your words by a split second.**
  If you feel yourself struggling to add a gesture to endorse something you said, drop it and do something else with your hands.

- **Talk to yourself in a full-length mirror.**
  If you're not naturally a body language chatterbox you could feel awkward when you do start endorsing your words with gestures. One small work-out every day will make you look and feel more confident.

- **Visualise yourself talking and gesticulating.**
  The imagination is a powerful tool and spending a few moments doing some virtual rehearsal will be almost as good as the real thing.

- **Congruence can also apply to group scenarios.**
  When you're with other people, sitting or standing like them is called postural congruence and can imply group uniformity or acceptance.

A BRIEF GUIDE TO INCONGRUENCE

Okay, who stepped out of line and who trod on whose toes? This is where your words are doing a tango, your vocal tone's waltzing while your body language is busy break-dancing. Your signals just don't match, which makes anyone watching think there's something fishy about your main point. You don't look as though you mean what you say. Even your own body's not convinced. I also call this type of body language Personal Heckling.

When your words, tone and body language all say different things it's incongruent. For the listener or audience this creates a state of cognitive dissonance – i.e. they receive conflicting signals and are unsure about which message to believe. For their own intellectual comfort they'll opt for the most reliable and this means it's the body language that they will usually assume to be the more honest communicator. We think it's harder to fix and rig, and in many ways we're probably right. The only variable is if the listener is keen to collude with the 'lie', in which case they will opt for whichever signals are giving out the message they want to hear. So a besotted lover could believe a partner who says they love them too, even though they're eyeing up someone else as they say it.

So, avoid sending incongruent signals. Or as somebody else said once: say it straight, or you'll get it crooked.

If your words aren't going to sit happily with your gestures you'd be better off not speaking at all because at best you'll look insincere and at worst you'll appear to be a liar. Imagine smirking when you tell someone you love them or staring wide-eyed in horror as you try to convince your best friend that you like her new hairdo! Think of this behaviour as your Personal Heckler.

Incongruent gestures can also be what are called ambivalent signals. This is where there's no desire to deceive but by saying one thing while your body language suggests another means that you are presenting both your conflicting thoughts to an audience, which can end up confusing them.

I once attended a presentation by a mind-numbingly dull speaker from the financial sector. If his brand of delivery could have been bottled and sold to hospitals it would have eliminated the need for an anaesthetist. This man was so dull even dishwater was trying to sue for libel. Somewhere around the end of his talk he decided to tell us that his company 'feel very passionate about our clients'. This flamboyant claim was accompanied by a deadpan expression and the very briefest of glances at the audience. If that was his idea of passion I just felt very sorry for his wife. While I didn't expect him to start dry-humping the light projector to add emphasis to his words I did expect a flicker of enthusiasm to light up his features. His incongruent delivery made a sham of the entire statement.

How to Avoid Incongruence

- **Try not to copy other people.**

  Although we all learn via imitation it is possible to be too obvious about 'borrowing' a signature gesture from somebody else. These are called absorbed actions. They might look good on them but appear phoney on you.

- **Video yourself speaking, both socially and professionally if you give talks in your job.**

  Spot the differences in delivery. Are you Jekyll and Hyde? Do you seem to be putting on an act? If so, spend time studying the more natural-looking signals and delete the rest from your repertoire.

- **Avoid using the poker-face technique.**
  By sitting very very still you'll never fool people into thinking you're more sincere as they'll just wonder what it is you're trying to hide. Small genuine movements are better than sitting like a statue.
- **Watch out for what's called non-verbal leakage.**
  This is the essence of incongruence, when your words say one thing but your smaller gestures signal something else entirely. Find out what your pet fiddles, or 'adaptors', are. Adaptors are those small self-comfort touches we do when we feel anxious or unsure. Do you fiddle with jewellery or your hair? Do you straighten your glasses more times than is necessary? Find other things to do with your hands as they could be giving the game away as you speak.

When you first begin to work on your own body language you'll find yourself doing what are called 'self-policing' movements. This is where you go to place your hand in your pocket but then quickly pull it out again because you don't feel the gesture is appropriate. This is a natural stage of learning but you need to move out of it as quickly as possible as it will imply incongruence. Try telling yourself what you *do* want your hands to do instead of what you *don't*.

Shortfall signals are those that appear to be an under-reaction to stimulus. For instance, you lose out on a job you wanted but sit poker-faced, wearing the slightest hint of a frown. Everyone knows you're seething inside and if this form of masking doesn't work it will look incongruent. Take yourself to the next level of honesty if you can, or leave the room to let rip out of ear-shot.

A BRIEF GUIDE TO OVERCONGRUENCE

This is when your words, tone and non-verbal signals are all in step – which is good – but you're trying too hard and getting carried away, which is bad. Your tone is too strong and your movements are too exaggerated. You look like a very bad conman. Or a politician. Nobody's *that* convinced about what they're saying. Take a cold shower and calm down. Come back when you can manage to look sincere.

Overcongruent communications are the enemy of sincerity, so avoid them at all costs. Cheesy doesn't sell unless you're employed by a TV shopping channel.

Also known as overkill signals, overcongruent deliveries are almost more of a pain. They used to be quite rare, apart from the odd TV boffin or *Blue Peter* presenter, but now the cult of overcongruence has reached a high street near you. It involves overdone gestures and facial gurning that squeeze the last breath of sincerity out of any communication.

Overcongruence is Tony Blair going misty-eyed and blinking back the tears over any subject matter that could be labelled 'a little bit sad'. It's Gordon Brown playing at a giant invisible piano as he stabs the air in a downward thrust with two index fingers as he talks about nothing very important. It's the girl at the check-out asking how you're feeling today with a fixed grin and it's the team leader who's jumping up and down like an overexcited cheerleader as he heads up yet another dreary, soul-rotting 'away day'.

Get it *too* right and you'll get it all wrong and people will hate you because, thanks to the likes of Jeremy Paxman, they can sniff out a phoney a mile off.

How to Avoid Overcongruence

- **Keep your hand gestures within the zone of congruence – i.e. between your shoulders and your waist.**
  The higher they get the less congruent you look.

- **Ask yourself: am I genuinely a wild and zany person with a barrel-load of enthusiasm for my subject?**
  If the answer is 'no' (and it's best to be honest) then tone it down several notches.

- **Get in front of that full-length mirror and work your way through a decreasing scale of body language wackiness.**
  Repeat this phrase: 'We sell the biggest products for the smallest prices' and try to look as though you mean it. Begin with wild arm-waving and work downwards until you're virtually immobile. Then work your way back up until you reach the level of movement that works.

A BRIEF GUIDE TO MASKING

But not all your body language will be about projecting your 'ideal' message. Unlike animals, humans spend a vast amount of time trying to suppress their negative signals. This suppression of thoughts and feelings is known as 'body language masking'. When animals mask they tend to do so for personal survival. Apes tend to mask pain and illness because in the wild any sign of weakness could lead to them being attacked. However, while most animals signal their other thoughts and emotions freely and honestly, inhibited humans prefer to throw a modesty-blanket around any spontaneous or instinctive displays. Like prudish Victorians covering up chair and table legs, humans go to great lengths to avoid flaunting any naked, raw emotion, unless it's during a football match, when all bets are off.

This emotional queasiness has made us all prolific verbal and non-verbal liars. We tell people we're fine when we're really feeling crap, we play it cool when we're drooling with lust or love, we blink back the tears at a funeral, we feign indifference when told we've been turned down for promotion or missed out on that top award, and we act out denial when our partner asks if they're losing their hair or turning into a lard-arse. Our entire lives have become a silent struggle between our animal, instinctive side and the strategic, social, human side of our nature. By masking our true feelings we feel somehow superior and more evolved.

How to Mask Effectively

- **Full-body masking is a hard stunt to pull off.**

  In general your biggest give-aways of true emotion will be your hands and your feet. Bring these in on the act or keep them out of trouble by doing something while you're masking. If a friend asks if you like his/her ghastly girl/boyfriend make sure you're zipping your boots or straightening your tie as you answer.

- **If you feel enormous pressure building before you mask, the best form of relief is the truth.**

  If your partner asks if you've forgotten their birthday, shouting: 'Yes, of course I did, I'm a cold-hearted unthinking git!' will clear the way for the following mask: 'Joking! Of course I didn't, I have a surprise present for later!'

- **Always analyse the reason for your mask before you apply it.**

  How hurtful would the truth be, or how damaging to your career or relationship? How hurt would your mother be if you tell her what you really think of that jumper she knitted for you? Or how detrimental would it be to your love life if you told your partner you'd had better sex with someone else? This could be a powerful motivator to create a convincing mask.

YOUR VERBAL VS NON-VERBAL SKILLS

If words are so unimportant when you're creating an effective communication, how come we've neglected our non-verbal skills? Like sex, body language expertise *should* just come naturally but – like sex – sadly, it rarely does. Animals don't need manuals to help them signal fear, fight or flirt, so why is the human animal, with all its great intellect, so confused and intimidated by non-verbal messages? How did we get so paranoid and puzzled by a process that is so simple it should be a joy?

The answer is that while animals coped well with body language, humans (as usual) decided to tinker around with what was already a perfectly decent system. Or to put it another way, we started to speak. Overcome with our own cleverness at inventing words, we then decided to stop using our eyes. In an effort to maintain social decorum and harmony, all kids from about the age of two years old are told that it's rude to stare. Great. Stop looking at other humans and stop reading their body language.

We then set about promoting words to the top of the communication pecking order. Thanks to the frenzied use of texts and email we like to pretend body language is as extinct as Victoria Beckham's puppy fat. But if that's true, why is it such a crucial factor in modern life? If words count more, then why do politicians bend over backwards to get their faces on TV or in the newspapers in a bid to win our votes? Why not just print transcripts of their speeches? Why do Hollywood stars still spend hours pouting and preening on the red carpet and why does job recruitment entail live interviews where your image will be scrutinised for much longer than your CV?

What is it that body language does that words just fail to do?

Texts and emails have caused a huge revolution in the way we communicate but their ability to communicate is limited. However many smiley faces and capitals we like to use, both text and email lack the ability to transmit genuine emotion. Like a speak-your-weight machine they tell us the facts but without the meaning or attitude. They're the modern version of semaphore or the telegram.

The same is true in face-to-face transactions. Imagine someone who talks in a monotone, using neither pitch nor gesture to make their point. If they walked into a room and said the building was on fire they'd have problems getting anyone to evacuate.

The point is that, as much as we choose to deny or ignore it, it's the non-verbal communication that we rely on when a message is high-importance, because when it comes to words alone we find it hard to understand, remember or believe what we're told.

Imagine you've taken a sickie from work. You've got to contact your boss to sell the lie that you're draped in the duvet because of 'something I ate'. How would you prefer to get that message across, by email, phone or video conferencing? The yellow-belly in you would plump for the email or the phone because you know your visual displays would let you down in a minute if you opted for face-to-face. If you chose the phone you'd very likely get someone else to do the call and then you'd have to go through the ritual of analysing the boss's response because you couldn't see them: 'Did she *really* sound as though it was okay?' 'Did he seem annoyed?' 'Are you *sure* she didn't sound sarcastic when she said she hoped I'd feel better soon?' 'When he said I should take as long off as I needed did he really mean I shouldn't bother going back at all?'

Words alone, i.e. emails and texts, are for lightweights, then. Although it's great to use email or text to dump your spouse, sack your employees or tell your bank manager where to get off it's mainly because your bottom is clenched so tight with fear that it looks as though it's been Botoxed.

Words are for windbags and worriers, too; people who feel that an email stands as 'proof of delivery' as though scared every message has a legal implication, or old-school politicians who think that verbal diarrhoea is the perfect antidote to a killer question from Jeremy Paxman.

Modern society is word-saturated, but being bombarded with too many words is not the same thing as having increased comprehension; in fact in reality it's quite the opposite. Neural pruning is the psychological term for your brain's own little spam filter. Too many words in the form of phone calls, emails, texts, business meetings and 'keynote' presentations or speeches just make our brains less attentive. Rather than adapting to absorb more information they've evolved to dispose of a vast majority of it, meaning we're throwing out some good along with the useless. We also use more jargon in an attempt to create shortcuts but the staleness of most jargon makes it a turn-off rather then a memory-jogger.

In many ways your words are like your holiday snaps. Ever look through someone else's holiday photos? How boring is that? The point is you had to be there. For the person who took them they're evocative of the whole experience but all you can see is a mangy-looking donkey or yet another dull old sunset.

In an important communication words are only a very poor representation of your thoughts and feelings.

WORDS THAT WORK

The only verbal communication in the workplace that rates as high-impact is gossip. Relate a rumour about the boss and her accountant and the whole office will be able to repeat the story a nanosecond later, but that's only because gossip is the modern version of story-telling and stories fix in the mind because they conjure up strong visual images (although possibly unwanted ones in the case of the boss and the accountant!). So even interesting verbal communications require strong visual images to back them up.

Straight talking is another way to get your point across unambiguously. Take as an example the master of verbal clarity, Simon Cowell. When confronted with yet another talentless singer on *Pop Idol*, Cowell might simply say, 'I'm sorry, I thought it was dull.' He might use words as weapons but at least he knows that there's very little room for misunderstanding after he's spoken.

When you text or email other people you will assume that their understanding of your selected words will be exactly the same as your own, but life proves that assumption wrong several times a day.

Keeping Cowell in mind, it's important you don't underestimate the measly 7 per cent that is verbal impact. Although our ears are fitted with their own spam filter, especially when we're hearing from parents, teachers, the office bore or a long-term partner going on about their day at work, some verbal communications do leap off the page and you should watch your words as well as your tone of voice.

WORD TEST – FINDING OUT WHY YOUR WORDS DON'T ALWAYS COUNT

Here's a test you *can* try at home to shock yourself into realising the low value of your verbal communication, especially when used in isolation.

Ask a friend, relative or partner to lie on the floor with their eyes closed. Then, using concise, step-by-step verbal commands, tell them how to get up. Each instruction must be gradual and specific and you mustn't use body language. You can't say 'roll over' or 'sit up' but you can say things like: 'move your hand 45 degrees to the left'. See how hard it is to form clear, precise, specific verbal communications without the non-verbal signals to explain them? It's the quickest way to spot the fact that what's in your head remains in your head. What you say only partially transcribes your thoughts. As you struggle with this exercise you'll begin to understand how non-specific your verbal communications are and how much we expect other people to read our minds.

Key Points:
- Remember that your verbal dialogues account for as little as 7 per cent of the perceived effect of your communication.
- To create a good message you need to be congruent, i.e. your words, tone and body language should all say the same thing.
- Work on boosting your word-power. Clear, concise speech is vital if you want to avoid creating 'dead' communication.

Now you've learnt the impact of non-verbal signals and why they play such an important role in everyday communications it's time to look at why we use them. To understand the psychology of body language signals we're going to take a look at ape behaviour and the lessons we all learn as children. If the 'why' of human behaviour doesn't interest you please flip to the more practical advice in Part Two (page 41). However, keep in mind that a deeper understanding of what prompts your behaviour will make change and improvement much more effective.

2

FROM MONKEY TO MAN

When did you first do body language? Approximately 15 minutes after you were born, that's when. The human animal is the only animal that is truly helpless straight after it's born. While other animals can fight or forage for food the human baby just lies back looking cute.

Your cuteness was good. In fact it was vital for your survival as it made older humans want to look after you. You also began to mirror the facial expressions of the adults around you to strengthen the bonding process. As you got older this became what's called learned behaviour as you happily mimicked anyone and everyone around you to get your messages across.

Most of the body language you use is learned behaviour, but some is more instinctive and part of your evolutionary processing. While the input from your parents, siblings and peers influences much of your behaviour, quite a lot of what you do goes much further back. A quick trip to the zoo could explain a lot about your current body language behaviour, especially in the workplace.

Your entire life is a constant struggle between your animal, instinctive side and your logical, strategic, social human side.

Although we consider ourselves light years away from the behaviour of apes it's impossible to suppress the instinct to fight for power, status, space, food and sex. In many ways your inner ape is still a very potent voice in your mind, but how does that affect your daily behaviour and body language?

Apes and other animals are primarily concerned with survival. As humans we still face daily risks but we've become immune to constant concerns about getting enough food or not getting beaten up by stronger humans. Although we have evolved a greater capacity for worry, fear and stress, it's mainly focused around trivia, like bin collections, crashing PCs and office politics. The things that make us 'go ape' tend to be things like road rage, trolley rage or even phone rage.

Like apes, our lives evolve around status, power and pecking orders, but unlike apes we place less emphasis on physical strength and power and more on career, class or financial-based status.

Like it or not, though, your animal instincts still play a major role in most of your body language signals. When stronger emotions occur, your inner ape starts to creep out. We've already seen the effect he has on your greeting rituals. Pulling back the lips is a signal of submission or acceptance for most apes and we've refined it into the smile of greeting, which is why we feel so angry when a colleague forgets to return the smile first thing in the morning. You've signalled you come in peace but he's given a noncommittal response. In animal terms it's as though he's chosen to leave his 'fight' options open. No wonder one of the biggest complaints I hear in corporate feedback is: 'I said good morning and smiled, but he ignored me.' Although this might sound trivial in business, in animal terms it is heavy stuff!

Alpha male apes display their authority by their physical stillness and their use of space, which is why Sir Alan Sugar stands out as the boss in *The Apprentice*. His huge desk and large chair create an ape-like signal of authority, as does his physical stillness while he allows the apprentices to squabble and chatter between themselves.

The royals employ these ape-like signals of status to useful effect. Diana was the only leading royal to use mirroring techniques, altering her own body language style to fit the patterns of others around her. For most of the royals this dropping of status would be unthinkable. The Queen is far more alpha male in mirroring terms, projecting a very constant sense of stillness and lack of physical empathy no matter who she's with.

Whereas alpha males project power through strength, stillness and space, alpha females are more likely to use grooming, food and nurturing to create their power base. Grooming is like gossip to apes, it creates empathy and rapport. Alpha females will groom other apes to pacify them and bond with them. They also use nurturing acts which they then use as a very potent bargaining tool. If another ape misbehaves the affection will be switched off until the naughty ape is back under control again. Sound familiar?

APE AGGRO

Animals fight over two key things: status and territory. Once the pecking order has been established, though, most colony members will respect it more or less because they know that a hierarchical set-up means their best chance of peace. This is also true of most offices: there's rarely a challenge to the boss's authority, no matter how draconian or unpopular he or she might be. This is because humans fear rocking the boat more than they fear living in a way that is unpleasant for them. The same fear affects politics. No matter how unpopular a leader might be, the fact that they're the leader makes them hard to unseat. Rival parties know that – as much as people like to moan or vote against them at local elections as a 'warning shot', when it comes to getting them out, the fear factor has to be taken into the equation.

Family set-ups are more prone to status challenges because once the kids are reared to the point where they can survive by themselves parental authority becomes virtually invalid. 'Because I said so' or 'Because you do what I say while you're under my roof' are verbal power tactics heard in houses across the land but they're usually little more than bluff. When the child is more determined and fearless than the parent (and possibly bigger and stronger too) there are very few ways to keep them in check.

AGGRESSIVE AROUSAL

In animals, and in humans, suppressed aggression leads to some interesting body language. When an ape feels threatened it will go through a state known as aggressive arousal. For humans this is where the automatic nervous system kicks in. The sympathetic nervous system creates a state that is good for fight, which means that the adrenalin starts to flow, your breathing patterns change, your muscles tense and your body hair stands on end. In apes and in humans this allows us to perform body language acts that are known as ritualised combat – i.e. threatening to attack in the hope that our apparent toughness will intimidate an opponent and make him/her back down.

Monkey to Man: Aggressive Arousal Signals in Human Form

When an ape might screech, strut and charge, your human ape state might display:

- Accelerated blink rate
- Shallow, rapid breathing
- A higher voice pitch
- Increased pulse rate
- Clenched teeth
- Clenched fists

RITUALISED COMBAT

In apes this takes the form of chest-banging, pacing and jumping up and down making a lot of noise. If that sounds familiar but you're having trouble placing it, just take a look at the football terraces when there's a needle match. Opposing fans use exactly the same kind of posturing to intimidate their rivals, sticking out their chests, pacing and shouting. Then come the ape-like mock attacks and odd little dance rituals to rev the whole crowd up. Usually the 'safer' the fans the more exaggerated their ape-like power-postures, so if there's a big show of police or officials everyone joins in the jeering but where there's the likelihood of a real fight the ritualised combat might be toned down.

Monkey to Man: Ritualised Combat Signals in Human Form

Where an ape might pace about, chest-bang or wave its arms your human ape might:

- Pace about
- Use chest-prod gestures
- Walk with arms held away from the side of the body
- Sport a puffed chest
- Frown
- Head-baton (jut their head forward as they speak)
- Finger point
- Wave fists
- Shout
- Place hands on hips
- Splay legs

DISPLACEMENT SIGNALS

If fight isn't an option, perhaps because the other ape is higher in status or just stronger or bigger, you'll often see an outbreak of displacement signals. This is where the aggression has to be suppressed out of fear. For an ape this can often lead to self-attacks, where the violence is turned inward out of frustration. The human animal has similar techniques, given the same circumstances. If you work with an overbearing colleague or a customer who gives you constant grief you could find you're taking the aggression out on yourself.

Monkey to Man: Displacement Signals in Human Form
Where an ape might hit itself or pull out its hair, the human ape might display:

- Nail-biting
- Finger-picking
- Hair-pulling

- Teeth grinding
- Aggressive scratching
- Chewing gum
- Punching own hand

DISTRACTION SIGNALS

And then there are the flirt or redirection signals. When an ape is being attacked it will often perform what looks like an entirely unrelated and counter-productive gesture, like yawning, grooming or scratching. Or it will even start to flirt. You probably think you know what this is all about. Humans flirt when they're with someone they fancy. But what about flirting at work? What about those people who turn on the charm with everyone in the place, male, female, young and old? Do they fancy everyone in the building? Are they corporate nymphomaniacs? Possibly, but probably not. Human flirting can be similar to ape flirt signals. And apes employ flirt signals as part of what's called a distraction process. Okay, so they flirt to have sex, but they also flirt to signal submission to a threatening ape. This flirting is pretty full-on industrial-strength stuff too, but it's not done to promote the sexual act, except in the bigger ape's mind. Faced with a muscle-bound ape a weaker ape will often bend over and stick its bottom in the air. This is to distract the stronger ape's mind from thoughts of violence and turn them towards sex instead. Only not with the submissive ape. It's a ploy. Just as a lot of workplace flirting is done as a ploy, to keep harmony at work and to help avoid conflict. Next time someone bats their eyelashes at you, flatters you or leans over your desk to reach for the stapler, remember it might not be so much about seduction as keeping the peace.

Monkey to Man: Distraction Signals in Human Form

Where an ape might stick out its bottom, the human version of distraction signals can be:

- Smiling with eye contact
- Extended touch in a handshake
- Eye up and down body appraisals
- Over-laughing at the boss's jokes
- Flirty emails
- Flattery about clothing, hair, scent or weight loss
- Proximity displays
- Exaggerated attention displays, even during periods of intense boredom

YOUR INNER CHILD

Let's move forward a few evolutionary cycles now to your own life as a child, where you learned body language for survival and reward. When you smiled everyone went ga-ga and when your face crumpled up for tears and screaming you saw adult faces turn fearful, giving you your first burst of baby-power.

From that moment on you used your body language to get whatever you wanted. Small children are egocentric, so this would have been the way your body language worked. If you needed food or attention you would have screamed or cried, going red in the face and pummelling the air with your fists. If the food that arrived didn't suit you, you would have wrinkled up your face in disgust and turned your head from side to side. Sulking would have meant folded arms, a dipped head and a jutting bottom lip. Your face would have happily contorted in jealousy if another kid had something you didn't.

If you lied you would have tried to cover your face with your hands and you would have thought nothing of throwing a tantrum wherever people gathered in a public place.

You also developed a very sophisticated system of calming and comforting yourself, too. You might have sucked your thumb or maybe rubbed at your cot blanket. At times you could have rocked in your chair or chewed at your toys.

Of course you've moved on now, right? I mean, it's not as though you'd sit at a board meeting sucking your thumb or throw yourself on to the floor of the boss's office to kick and scream when that pay rise gets turned down.

Manipulative Rituals

You will have realised by now that I'm about to tell you that whether you know it or not you're still performing many of these gestures and patterns of body language behaviour. Maybe you don't suck your thumb any more but I bet there's some kind of substitute that goes into your mouth when you're placed under pressure. Would a grown man stick his lower lip out in a sulky pout when things weren't going his way? Take a look at José Mourinho and Simon Cowell, both of whom have turned bottom-lip-jutting into an art form.

Many of these baby or childlike displays are what is called pseudo-infantile re-motivators, meaning you look helpless or vulnerable in a bid to motivate someone else to be kind, non-critical or even nurturing.

Self-Comfort Gestures

Like it or not you'll have retained many of your baby body language gestures for use throughout your life. They become self-comfort gestures, like fiddling or self-strokes that we all perform to stimulate a state of happiness or relaxation; aggressive gestures like slamming down phones or stomping out of the room when we don't get our own way, or even childlike manipulative gestures, attempting to look cute, sweet and submissive when we want to be liked or to get someone to do something for us.

Both your inner child and your inner ape are still very much in charge when it comes to your body language signals. Being aware of these influences is vital if you're going to tailor your bodytalk to get the most out of situations, otherwise your communications will remain deeply incongruent – i.e. your words, tone and non-verbal signals will be hugely out of kilter at moments when it matters.

From Baby to Adult

As a child did you…?	As an adult do you…?
Suck your thumb	Suck or chew pens
	Smoke
	Mouth-touch or stick your fingers in your mouth
Go quiet or hide	Fold your arms
	Touch your face or perform a partial face-cover
	Hunch your shoulders
	Stick your hands into your pockets
	Avoid eye contact
Cry	Jut out your bottom lip or jaw under pressure
	Rub your fingers or knuckles over your eyes
	Pull your hair over your face
	Perform mouth-shrugs instead of smiling
	Speak very loudly

Throw tantrums	Slam down phones
	Use noisy gestures, like punching the desk or clicking your pen
	Run your hands through your hair
	Scratch or pat the top of your head
	Purse your lips
	Stare

ADULT BODYTALK

Once your frontal lobes started to develop you learnt to share and use empathy, and you also started to be less self-obsessed and more tuned in to the wants and needs of others. You began to be strategic in your behaviour, too, looking at long-term results rather than just living in the here and now.

Currently your behavioural choices are governed by three key factors or 'voices':

1   **Your instinctive voice or your inner ape.**
    This voice will steer you towards instant gratification rewards, e.g. I want, I get and to hell with the consequences! This is your inner warrior or your inner wimp, depending on the situation. It thinks quickly and it acts even faster. You might think you've contained it but it has a habit of leaking out via some of your smaller but deadlier body language signals, letting other people know how you're *really* feeling.

2   **Your social voice or your inner diplomat.**
    This is your adult voice, the one that thinks long-term and thinks empathetically. It knows the difference between short- and long-term gain in a situation and it will steer you towards the latter. In body language terms

it is the supreme masker, hiding all those instinctive gestures like snarling, scowling, sulking and staring, and replacing them with a sunny smile and a stiff upper lip.

3 **Your logical voice.**

This is your inner computer, churning out facts and figures and clear thinking, that bypasses emotions and sticks to the detail instead. In some people this voice is an underperformer but in others it sits centre-stage, creating low levels of body language activity and high levels of android-style movement.

Your instinctive voice shouts quickest and loudest but – often purely for personal survival – you've learnt to temper it and to mask its non-verbal signals. What this means is that your body language is a bit of a mongrel, the result of all three voices trying to be heard at the same time.

Let's take an over-the-counter scenario. You work in a shop and you're facing the customer from hell. They're demanding and rude and they've just asked to try on their sixteenth pair of shoes. Your inner ape is telling you to stick that pair of shoes where the sun don't shine but your social inner diplomat is explaining that he is just a careful shopper who is suffering from stress because he has had a hard week. He doesn't mean to be rude, he's just taking it out on the nearest person around. Meanwhile your logical voice is informing you in a very patient tone that smacking this customer around the face will create a scenario involving a sacking and probably the police. It's reminding you about your mortgage and the need to keep this job to ensure you have a roof over your head.

Now, rewind the scene. These voices are in your head. But what's going on with your body language as a result?

Well, your social voice has slapped a smile on your face to make you look customer-friendly. However, your inner ape has made that smile just a bit too rigid. The lips are pulled back in a rictus, which is a signal of attack rather than affection. Your social voice makes you nod while you listen to the customer's complaints but your instinctive ape has turned your hands into white-knuckled fists and your teeth are clenched so hard you can hardly get the words 'no problem' out.

Without even realising it, the customer from hell edits these mixed messages and – without even understanding the complicated process being used – deletes all the empathetic signals on display and only reacts to the ape-warrior ones. They accelerate their own aggressive displays or they storm across to report you to the manager.

Key Points:

- Body language accounts for over half the perceived impact of your communication.
- Body language has a higher credibility rating than your words – if your words and your gestures send out mixed messages it's the body language that the listener will believe.
- Body language isn't a precise science – each gesture can have many meanings.
- You're already a bit of an expert on body language – you've been doing it since you were 15 minutes old.
- Much of your body language is affected by your inner child and your inner ape!

PART TWO: PRACTICAL BODY LANGUAGE

The following chapters are all about you and about maximising your image to create success in your life. We're going to look at general tips and training here while specific situations and scenarios will come later in the book.

This is going to take some effort on your part. I hope you don't mind. No pain, no gain, as they say. We're going to have fun and we'll have a few fights but I promise you the effort will be worth it.

The first physical steps you're going to take in this book are all to do with maximising your own impact by changing your body language 'state'. This is where *The Body Language Bible* stops being just an interesting read and starts to become an exercise manual.

3

HOW TO MAKE YOUR BODY LANGUAGE WORK FOR YOU

While it's always fascinating to discover why we do what we do it's a whole lot tougher to take all that information and use it to help make changes. Change is vital though, as it's the only way to achieve body language excellence. Change will be challenging, but change is the paving that forms the path to charisma. If we're going to press on with this metaphor I might also add that self-consciousness, embarrassment and laziness are the slippery slime and mossy stuff that can make you skid or stall.

One piece of advice: when you're making changes, always keep your goals in mind. When you learnt to drive you were thinking about all the freedom your car would give you. When you look up a route on a map you take time to study the roads because you know exactly where they're leading. Dogs know there's some treat involved for good behaviour, like a biscuit or bone. If you feel you're changing your body language for the sake of it it'll be like taking driving lessons knowing you'll never own a car. So visualise the 'new you' before you start tweaking your gestures and focus on all the benefits that being body language literate are going to bring you.

THE BLINK FACTOR – ANALYSING AND EVALUATING YOUR OWN FIRST IMPRESSIONS

How quickly will other people be assessing you? Probably in the amount of time it takes to blink. When you walk into a room there will be an animal impulse for others in that room to assess you visually, even if they barely appear to be paying attention.

This impulse is part of the fight/flight survival response. The first information those others will need to obtain is whether you appear to constitute a threat or not. After that, though, it's a bit of an image free-for-all as they try to discover your status, job, reason for being there, sexual desirability, etc. And this isn't just for people you're meeting for the first time. In business the blink factor is ongoing. Every day you'll be viewed with these same eyes as people try to judge your mood or your leadership qualities, your knowledge or ability to either take control or be submissive, or their chances of getting you to work late, get coffee, explain the workings of the IT system, take all that flirting and saucy email stuff further when you cop off down the pub.

The Blink

Your 'blink' signals come from any or all of the following:

- Your gaze or eye contact
- Your posture
- Gestures
- Facial expression
- Touch
- Spatial behaviour
- Grooming (including your smell!)
- Dress

How many of these key factors do you think you're consciously aware of each time you meet people or walk into a room or an office? Here are a few quick questions:

- Do you know what your facial expression looks like or do you *feel* it and assume it's doing okay?
- Do you take a moment to stand tall and look relaxed before you walk into a room? Or do you shuffle in hoping no one's noticed you?
- Do you have an eye for grooming details? Are your nails always clean and nail varnish unchipped? Or do you sometimes rush out of the house hoping no one will notice or that if they do they'll think it's part of your boho chic look?
- When you speak do your hands ever get out of control? Are you always being told you wave your arms around too much? Do your hands tend to carry on their own conversations regardless of the fact that you're willing them to keep still?
- Are you aware of your own personal tics, fiddles, mannerisms or other habits that get worse when you're put under pressure?
- Do you ever make a conscious effort to keep your hands under control by shoving them into your pockets, clasping them behind your back or folding your arms?
- Do you ever use a handbag or pen as a prop to keep your hands occupied?
- Are you aware how close you stand to other people when you're talking?
- Do you give good shake? Are you sure your handshake is a good one and do you know exactly when to use it or when to instigate it?

- Do your feet ever tap or twitch when you're sitting down? Or does your leg swing or twitch?
- Do you evaluate your own eye contact, using more at times to create a positive impression, or do you allow it to be steered by your emotions, using less when you feel lacking in confidence or intimidated by a stronger character?

PRACTICAL STEPS TO THE PERFECT BODY LANGUAGE PERFORMANCE

Here is the first key thing you need to know about working on your own body language to enhance your impact and maximise your success:

Step One: Know Your Goal(s)

If you were about to shoot a gun you'd be given three basic commands:

READY

TAKE AIM

FIRE!

The order of these three words is simple but vital to ensure you hit your target. But how do you currently communicate?

READY...

FIRE!

...um...take aim?

The success rate of this approach is about the same as the success rate of firing a gun before you've aimed and expecting to hit the target. Apart from anything else, it's dangerous!

Speaking before you think is a common problem, and the thing about our communications and transactions is that often we don't bother to aim them before we fire. We're a bit flaccid about our target-planning. Our body language aiming is especially suspect. We don't get to see our own body language and so we tend to just let it do its own thing. Like an overindulged child, though, it starts to become a bit of a liability.

When did you last 'take aim' with your body language? If you've had a difficult transaction, or communication, with time for planning and preparation I bet you spent any prep time working out *what* to say rather than *how* to say it. Or how about approaching someone you fancy? There are loads of articles in lads' mags extolling the virtues of different chat-up lines but few that describe how a bloke should stand if he wants to impress a girl.

Like every other aspect of a transaction, your body language needs to be fine-tuned in keeping with your goal(s).

There are four different types of image goals for you to target:

- *The 'lifetime achievement' goal:* the image you want to project to others on a regular and long-term basis.
- *The strategic goal:* flexing your image and impact to suit a short-term set of circumstances.
- *The professional goal:* adopting a corporate or more professional image that matches your chosen career.
- *The role goal:* adopting differing images to suit your different life roles and responsibilities, like parent, daughter, wife, team-player, friend etc.

If you understand your goals you will be well on the way to understanding how to maximise your body language techniques to achieve them. If you suffer from goal-confusion, though, you're destined to look something of a prize chump.

Before you attend an important meeting or scenario spend a few moments creating specific image goals for that meeting. Ask yourself:

- How do I want to be perceived?
- If I were wearing a T-shirt with words printed across the front to describe me and my personality, what would I want those words to say?
- What body language can I use to get those words across?

Spend a few more moments visualising those words. To do this you can work on very basic body language rules and knowledge. For instance, if one T-shirt word is 'confident', visualise people you know who look confident and then see yourself acting in the same way. This technique is a great learning tool for body language as it replicates the system you used to learn how to move and gesticulate in your childhood: play and mimicry.

As a basic ploy you can create a simple body language tool-kit that will make instant improvements, like:

If your target quality is confidence
Your body language tools are:
- Steady eye contact
- Upright posture
- Open gestures
- A relaxed facial expression
- Your smile

If your target quality is friendliness

Your body language tools are:

- Smiling
- Nodding
- A warm handshake
- Softened eye expression
- Standing face-on to the other person

If your target quality is status or leadership

Your body language tools are:

- A firm handshake
- Good eye contact
- Straight posture
- Sitting centrally or at the front
- No fiddling or wriggling
- Smooth, emphatic gestures

If your target quality is calm

Your body language tools are:

- Measured breathing
- Smooth, synchronised body movements
- Lowered shoulders, not tensed or hunched
- No fiddling
- Sitting back in your seat
- Elbows on the arms of the chair
- Hands lightly clasped

Does modifying your body language like this make you a liar? Shouldn't you just 'be yourself'? Isn't this conning people and acting false or not being true to type?

Honing or changing your body language signals is part of a

natural process. You learnt most of it by imitation and there's nothing wrong with adding to your repertoire. You'd feel happy about learning new words to express yourself so why not new gestures?

Another fact of body language is that when you feel that you're 'being yourself' you probably aren't. Most people I coach are mortified when they first see their own body language on CCTV because it's not what they thought they were doing and not what they intended to say. They make changes because they're not putting the right message across.

One of the key changes I made to my own body language was to stop looking shy. I am shy and I feel shy but shyness doesn't work in my job. Worse still, it was getting misinterpreted. People assumed I was being stuck-up or arrogant.

Step Two: Play to Your Strengths

When you target your image goals make sure you pick the right set of competencies. Look at your own USPs (unique selling points) and try to enhance them, rather than suppressing or deleting them. Tweaking is good but industrial-strength masking is not. It's hard to perform and the cracks will start to show.

Here's how your body language works as a communication tool:

- You talk to someone.
- While you're talking you gesticulate or pull a face.
- They see you do this.

So far, so simple. But of course the whole process is far more complex than that. What happens next is something called 'cognitive algebra', which is the term used to describe the following process of assessment via visual recognitions:

1 **Stage one: scanning**

   This is when you're being generally looked at. You employ a gesture. Let's say you fold your arms. This is the stage called 'creating stimulus'. You did it, they saw it. If the pair of you went to court you could both swear on a stack of Bibles that's what you did.

2 **Stage two: focusing**

   Your 'listener' starts to take notice, consciously analysing the stimulus you've produced.

3 **Stage three: comprehension**

   Consciously or subconsciously the 'listener' searches for meaning in what you did. What is this gesture telling them? That you're cold? Or angry? Are you nervous? Or have you just realised you forgot to wear underwear? By now the communication has gone out of your control.

4 **Stage four: assimilation**

   Your listener starts to link what they have seen to memories. This is the conscious evaluation process. Based on previous experiences of your gesture your listener is going to make judgements on your personality or mood. The listener is rummaging through their memory banks to form connections, meaning they're trying to create understanding by relating this to a time when they've seen this gesture before and remembering what it meant when they did. As you can gather, this is a very flawed way of assimilating information, especially when it comes to body language. What if they have poorly evaluated their past experiences?

5 **Stage five: response**

   This could be along the lines of: 'I had a teacher once who always folded her arms when she was telling me off. I therefore dislike this man because I feel he's being dictatorial and domineering.' Or: 'I always cross my arms when I'm feeling nervous or unsure. I feel sorry for this guy and I'll do my best to make him feel at ease.'

This is why it's so important to evaluate your own body language signals and make some effort to understand their effect on other people. If you're aware that folding your arms could create the impression that you're standoffish or even aggressive you can begin to make moves to improve the quality of your signals, either by *not* folding your arms at all, ever, or you could minimise any negative connotations by balancing your gestures to create harmony.

Playing to your strengths means knowing your USPs and capitalising on them. When you work on your image make sure you're accentuating the positives and masking any negatives. Fit the qualities to the situation and avoid working strictly on assumption – e.g. 'I know that client likes me because I always speak my mind.' Maybe they like you *despite* the fact you speak your mind. Or: 'I'll never attract that guy, I get much too nervous when he talks to me.' Perhaps it's your diffidence that attracted him in the first place. Did you never go for the shy guy above all the mouthier lads?

How to self-assess

- If you're not sure of your core image strengths, ask people you trust.
- Ask as many people as possible and find out what they first thought of you when they met you.
- Compile your own list of descriptive words and try to discover why people came to those conclusions. I promise

you'll be surprised if the people you ask choose to be honest. This is a very valuable exercise but must be done in an open way with no stress or pressure.

- Never start arguing with people's opinions or becoming defensive. If you do, you'll find the evaluation process will break down rather quickly.

Step Three: How to Work Through Body Language Change

Assessing your own body language is hard because catching yourself unawares is as physically impossible as tickling yourself. (A brief pause to give all those of you who didn't know you couldn't tickle yourself a chance to try.)

In perception terms you are either aware of your own body language or very unaware. Once you become aware you also become inhibited, which has an instant and traumatic effect on your gestures and movements, altering them out of all recognition. Take my word for it, I know this to be true. The minute I tell people what I do for a living their muscles undergo a form of rigor mortis and their movements become more wooden than the entire cast of *Thunderbirds*.

Nevertheless, tweaking your own body language to create improvement is so absolutely necessary that you're going to have to move through the pain barrier and launch yourself on a voyage of self-discovery. Why the pain? Because very few people are naturally gifted body language performers. A lot of people have the body language charisma rating of a sea urchin. When you start to become observant of your own behaviour you will find it's like looking at party snaps: embarrassing and depressing. You'll fail to recognise yourself or identify with your gestures, facial expressions and nervous tics and twitches. You'll wonder aloud why no friend has told you about this before.

You'll stop laughing at Gordon Brown and Mr Bean and start to feel empathy instead.

Not all the changes you're going to make will be traumatic; in fact the good news is that very few of them are, unless you're going to be a wuss.

What's a body language wuss? Well, they're those people who turn up on my courses to work on their body language but who then – like the runt of the litter at the school gym – produce a sick note.

By 'sick note' I don't mean a written letter from their mummy explaining why they don't have to join in; instead I'm talking about a series of verbal sick notes explaining why they do what they do in body language terms.

Instead of simply moving towards improved non-verbals they prefer to stall by explaining *why* they do what they do, as in: 'I only play with the change in my pocket because I'm nervous. I can't help it' or: 'I couldn't help frowning when my colleague walked in, it wasn't rudeness it's just the way my face goes.'

These are sick notes. You crossed your arms because you were cold, not to create a barrier from the person talking to you. You drummed your fingers out of anxiety, not boredom. It was shyness that prevented you from using eye contact, not rudeness.

The problem with body language sick notes is that we can't go through life handing them out. With your visual image you only really get the one shot. People will sum you up in as long as it takes to blink an eye, and if you look hostile or pointless then that's how they will think you are. If you're lucky and have more time they might discover the 'real' you buried under all that dodgy-looking rubble, but the big problem with modern life is we see way too many people per day to go rooting around for any hidden gems.

People tend to read by what they see and are often too busy to look for alternative reasons or causes. They get what they'll call a gut reaction about you and no amount of excuses will make up lost ground.

Anyway, when did you last apologise verbally for your own body language? If your partner accuses you of giving him or her a dirty look do you apologise and say you had an eyelash in your eye or do you shrug it off, assuming it's their problem if they misread your signals?

I yawned recently in a client meeting. We all know what that signals and – although in this case the boredom factor was teetering towards the unbearable – the only reason for my yawn was that I'd seen someone else yawning in an office across the way. Yawning is contagious, but try telling that to a client who thinks you've just been hugely disrespectful!

Body Language Bible Rule 1: No Sick Notes!

Don't make excuses to yourself. If it ain't working, fix it. The only thing that matters about your body language is how it's perceived and read by the people who matter to you. Strive to get it right first time; you might not get a second chance.

Body Language Bible Rule 2: You Can Change Your Behaviour!

Hurrah! There's no need for you to keep on fiddling with your cuffs or twiddling your hair every time you speak. There's no law of nature that says you can't do something else, like use some fabulous emphatic gestures instead. It's your choice, honestly! It takes 21–30 days to change a habit. After that you'll barely remember what it was you used to do.

Easy Tweaking

The really good news for you is that I will give you some easy tweaking tips that will have a huge effort/reward ratio, meaning you'll make some seemingly small changes with a hugely positive and potentially life-changing effect. I always claim that most politicians are only two body language tweaks away from looking human, it's just that either nobody seems to give them advice or they choose not to take it.

Most of my trainees turn up with worrying problems, like years of being passed over for promotion, being ignored at business meetings or getting feedback from their manager that their personal impact is negligible. You might think it would take months of counselling and coaching to create changes in their behaviour that are profound enough to have an effect, but not a bit of it. Often it's embarrassingly easy to pick out where they're going wrong.

Take a guy I was coaching from the food industry, who wanted to have more impact with his customers. Although he communicated quite well I noticed that when he mentioned any of his products his voice dropped and he mimed packet size rather than foodstuff. He even referred to them as 'units'. He also used what is called a very telling micro-gesture by which I mean his facial features changed into something like an expression of disgust or dislike when he referred to them. He was totally unaware of all this non-verbal signalling. The client would also have been unaware, but only consciously. Subconsciously the message received would have been that the product was crap. By coaching him to lose the facial micro-gesture and to mime something related to the product rather than its packaging I was able to change his impact as well as his sales figures. It's not always that easy, but the point I'm making is that small tweaks can have big results.

Then there will be the bigger changes. By this I mean habits you've had from birth and possibly beyond. These gestures, movements and rituals will have been with you so long they'll feel like part of your personality, but they're not. What they are is just behaviour, remember?

Body Language Bible Rule 3: Be Prepared To Get Out Of Your Comfort Zone

---

And here's the rub: by choosing to change your body language signals you *will* be tip-toeing outside your comfort zone. Awareness of your own movement creates a good deal of discomfort in itself. Recognising that some of the things you currently do make you look like a bit of a prat doesn't make for happy thoughts, either. And pushing your body through changes will make going back to a state of blissful ignorance and unconscious error very, very tempting.

But here's the thing: if you're prepared to shelve your dreams and goals in life for the sake of a little physical discomfort you're a wuss. What we're talking about here is a different kind of sick note. They are the sick notes you send to yourself to give you reasons for quitting. In essence they'll sound much the same as the 'why I broke my diet' or 'why I had that cigarette after I'd decided to give up' sick notes, all mainly trivial stuff that sounds even more trivial in retrospect.

So here's the deal: if you want to make excuses to yourself about why you should go on producing low-impact or poor-quality body language messages that could well be scuppering your career and your love life then you're a ninny and a milksop and you need to put this book down right now and go back to *The Lady* or *The Idiot's Guide to Cross-stitch* or something because we're about to part company at this juncture.

It might occur to you that I'm sounding a bit bossy right now. If so, you're absolutely right. What else did you expect? Would you hire a personal fitness trainer and then tell them you don't want to put in any physical exertion to get fit? Or tell Gillian McKeith that you didn't mind losing weight as long as you didn't have to give up your ten-burgers-a-day habit? Bossy is entirely appropriate at this stage of the book. Once you start to show you can work hard and once your body language begins to improve I'll start to sound nicer and we can be friends.

This chapter has shown how you are judged by other people, and how you're analysed subliminally. This has alerted you to the reasons why it's so important for you to make appropriate changes to your body language 'state'.

You've also been motivated into moving forward! And remember – no sick notes!

Key Points:
- Be aware of your blink factor – what do your first impressions say about you?
- Start by goal-planning.
- Create small tool-kits of behaviour for specific situations.
- Know your strengths and USPs.

4

A BEGINNER'S GUIDE TO POSTURE

In this chapter you'll be working on your own body language signals, as well as discovering some new tricks and techniques to make sure you're marketing yourself to the max. This is the key work-out section of the book, a kind of body language gym where you can start to hone your skills and increase your competency.

THE ULTIMATE POWER POSE

This simple but effective technique will form the basis of all the rest of the work you're going to do. In body language terms it's a one-size-fits-all. This realignment technique will be appropriate whatever your circumstances. It creates a perfect springboard for all your other gestures and signals. Get this one wrong and you'll never get the other stuff right.

There are two very good bits of news about doing this:

1   It's quick and easy.
2   It will affect the way you feel.

Changing Your State

You can use your posture to motivate, invigorate, uplift and even nourish yourself. The Power Pose you're about to do will make you look better, feel healthier and grow in confidence and self-esteem. It's an instant body language make-over.

Let's take a look at your 'normal' posture. How do you normally stand or sit?

- Are you straight-backed or stooped?
- Do you pull your shoulders forward in a self-protective gesture or stretch your chest wide, looking confident or confrontational?
- How do you stand or sit when you're under pressure? Does your posture become more compliant or more arrogant? Do you curl up or does your chest widen out?
- How do you stand or sit when you're tired or depressed? Do you slump more? Do you lie with your knees pulled up?

Power Posing is part of the techniques called changing your state. By looking more confident you'll start to feel more confident. Body language affects your emotional and mental well-being hugely. It's hard to look positive and feel down at the same time. The latest psychological thinking states that putting your best face forward is much more important than previously thought. Although we in the UK have a cultural history of 'keeping a stiff upper lip' this has been ridiculed or even described as dangerous by American psychologists who tend to adhere to the principle of 'letting it all hang out' rather than suppressing yourself emotionally.

So we started to follow suit, bawling at the first opportunity and displaying the full range of our inner misery, anxiety and stress at will. And then – guess what? We're now told that actually putting on a 'best face' of the type you'd use with strangers when you're trying to be polite is really good for you! It makes you feel better! The act is self-prophesying! What you look like is what you feel.

Powering Up

Now that I've sold you on Power Posturing you're about to feel cheated. Why? Because it's so darned easy. Virtually effort-free, in fact. You'll wonder how something so basic can also be so life-changing. You'll think I over-promised by telling you it will make you feel better, look better, lose weight and pull a partner. You'll think 'no pain, no gain' and wonder if I'm selling snake oil. But try it. It really does work. No one says everything good has to be hard to do.

Get yourself in front of a full-length mirror. If possible, find a place where you can see your back and side views too. Stand nude or in your under-crackers (unless you're doing it in a public place of course, but I suggest you'll feel safer in the privacy of your own bathroom or bedroom).

Stand normally. And I mean *normally*, no cheating.

Now, take these ten simple steps:

1 Pull yourself up to full height by stretching your spine as though you're trying to touch the ceiling with the top of your head. This will make you look at least half a stone lighter.

2 Keep your head straight, so that your chin is held at a right angle.

3 Wriggle your toes to make yourself feet-aware. Your feet are your power base, like the roots of a tree. If your feet

aren't 'well-planted', e.g., you're wearing wobbly high heels or your body weight is unevenly distributed because you're shifting between one foot and the other or your legs are crossed, then you're depleting your own personal power dramatically. I'm no fan of sensible shoes but it's possible for women to wear boots or well-balanced shoes that create a feeling of power. A higher heel can add to this perceived self-confidence but please steer clear of anything that makes you teeter about. Men's shoes are designed for proper power-walking but women tend to wear shoes that aren't practical. This adds to the perception of inequality and an unequal power/status balance in the workplace. Stand with your body weight evenly balanced on your feet.

4 Roll your shoulders in a circle, upward first and forward, then back and down. Keep them in the back and down position.

5 Allow your fingertips to brush against the side of your thighs.

6 Subtly push your lower pelvis forward a little so that your spine is completely straight. This entails pushing your bottom in and under. (Men should be rather more subtle with this move than women.)

7 Take a deep breath in, then allow all the air to be expelled from your lungs in a slow exhale.

8 Pull your stomach in.

9 Re-align your shoulders in case they've slumped as you exhaled.

10 Smile!

Look in the mirror again. How do you look? How do you feel? Better? More positive? How long did that take? A couple of seconds? I told you it was easy. Now all you've got to work out is how to get that charismatic posture in motion so you can get off to work.

YOUR POLE POSITION

I am no fan of over-choreographed body language but in this book I shall be coaching you to be charming. Please don't confuse charm with smarm. Charm is a genuine component of charisma. *Smarm* is something else though. Smarm means using overcongruent body language, falling over yourself to impress or be liked. We'll find out more about charm in later chapters but for the moment just keep the thought in your head that *smarm* is illegal, at least according to the laws of *The Body Language Bible*.

Forget being too perfect, then.

Body Language Bible Rule 4: Getting It All Right Means Getting It Wrong

---

However, that doesn't mean you shouldn't get it at least half right.

I always impress on people that it's a very good idea to at least *start* right with your body language. I call this getting into pole position. Start well and finish better but start well and go slowly downhill and at least you'll know they saw you looking good during the blink, or first impression. Start badly and go downhill and you might as well give up.

Get in front of the full-length mirror again, only this time take a prop with you. Your prop for pole position training will be a chair, only don't use it yet because we're going to do the standing stuff first.

Posture

I hope you know how to stand. If you don't then you're either a spectacular drunk or you have a serious couch potato habit.

But how do you feel about standing when people are looking at you? What about when you stand to make that business presentation or wedding speech, or to chat to that girl you fancy in the bar? Suddenly standing isn't so easy any more because you feel self-conscious. By creating a standing 'pole position' you can rehearse a pose beforehand, meaning you won't feel awkward at all next time it happens.

- Stand normally and look at your reflection. How do your hands feel? Are you using barrier gestures like folded arms or clasped hands to make you feel more comfortable? Then unclasp them. Let your arms hang by your sides as you did with your Power Pose.
- Now, think feet. No need to look down at them because that will just make you feel off-balance, just think of them instead. Get the weight of your body firmly balanced between the sole and the heel of your foot. And keep your weight right down the middle of each foot, too. Stand with your feet about shoulder-width apart (less for women) and have your toes pointing either straight or slightly outwards.
- Now work on your legs. Straighten them but don't make them so rigid that your knees lock.
- Pull your spine straight, your shoulders back and down and tilt that pelvis slightly forward as you did in your Power Pose.
- Look at your arms and hands in the mirror. These will need some working on. Try to pick a position where they look good, rather than one where they just *feel*

comfortable. Your ideal pole position might be so alien to you that it feels odd, but I promise this feeling will vanish after you've been doing it for a while. You body needs to learn what's called muscle memory, which means it gets used to the feeling of a new movement.

There is no one-size-fits-all with your arms and hands, which is why I'm not going to be overly prescriptive. A lot depends on your body shape, your arm-length, the size of your belly, etc. If you're tubby with short arms it's no good me telling you to clasp your hands in front of your body because this is going to look downright silly. If you're skinny and long-limbed like me you'll have arm-length to spare but then you might end up in the fig-leaf pose, which for men means hands clasped across the genitals, which is not a good look unless you're defending a free kick in footie.

You can try out a variety of hand/arm poses. Once you see how daft most of them look you'll be glad you put in some practice now, rather than halfway through that business presentation or chat-up line. I'll be giving you more specific tips in the next few chapters, coaching you through killer moments like business meetings or social events, but for now just make sure you've got at least one pose that works. Then it's up to you to keep using it until it both feels and looks natural and comfortable.

Now's the time to bring your prop in. Pull that chair in front of the mirror and sit down. Your second pole position needs to be done sitting down because that's the way you usually communicate in meetings.

You'll need to work on two sitting pole positions, one for a chair with arms and one without. The second option is the more challenging because it makes your arm movement more limited.

- Sit into the back of the chair unless you're so small this means your feet dangle off the ground. If this happens sit forward until they touch the floor.
- Straighten your back and don't slump.
- Either cross your legs at the thigh (for a man or a woman) or sit with them slightly open (if you're a man).
- If your chair has arms, rest your elbows on the arms, with your hands loosely clasped in front of you. If the arms are too wide apart, rest one elbow on one arm and let your other elbow rest on your leg so that your hands can be loosely clasped.
- If your chair is armless, clasp your hands loosely and place them in your lap.
- Or try resting one elbow on the back of the chair, with your arms clasped loosely. (This is quite casual so not for formal occasions.)
- And watch that hand clasp. You can mesh your fingers or just place one hand lightly over the other but don't use a tight clasp or do what's called *finger-steepling*, by which I mean pointing some fingers into a V-shape, either aimed at your own chin or towards the person you're talking to. I'll explain why not later in the book but for now I'll just say it can make you look very arrogant.

Power Walking

Now that you've perfected the art of standing and sitting (your key pole positions that will get you started) it's time to get your coordination going sufficiently to walk.

Sounds easy? You've been walking since you were a toddler – how hard can it be? The problem is you've been walking without thinking about it. Your walk techniques have been subconscious, reproduced on a regular basis by your muscle

memory. Now's the time to drag the skills kicking and screaming into the conscious mind, which will make you feel
uncomfortable, awkward and too self-aware.

Like all your bodytalk, though, it's vital that you're aware of
the current reality. If your walk is 'ideal' you're very lucky and
very much in the minority. Did you ever people-watch from a
window, studying people as they walk down the road? How
many walks looked okay and how many were in dire need of
urgent re-structuring? Grab a pair of your oldest, most well-
worn shoes from the wardrobe. Take a glance at the heels. How
are they worn? What angle are they at? Do you have a chip out
at the back, or are the sides worn at an angle? This should begin
to give you a clue about your own alignment.

I spent several years as a catwalk model and several more
years teaching models – including Naomi Campbell – how to
walk. Very few people have what I would call a naturally good
walk and some of the top catwalk models had to have their
entire walk pulled to pieces before being reconstructed into
something that looks fabulous but effortless.

So – get in front of that full-length mirror again, only this
time stand as far back as possible. Get into your Power Posture
pose (stretched spine, dropped shoulders, chin level, etc).

- Tuck your pelvis in and under (less so for the guys!).
- Allow your arms to hang loosely by your sides, keeping
  them slightly to the back.
- Keep looking straight ahead. It might feel as though you
  need to look at your feet but this will have a negative
  effect on your balance.
- Extend your right foot, placing your right heel lightly
  down on to the floor.

- Begin to peel off your left foot, keeping your weight over that foot, rather than tilting forward and leading with your head.
- Let your arms swing very slightly with the left arm coming forward at the same time as your right leg.
- Keep your pace slightly smaller than usual.
- Keep walking, coordinating all these movements until they become smooth and natural-looking.

If you're trying this work-out you might be thinking that it could take ten years or more before this all starts to look natural. Two vital tips here:

Body Language Bible Rule 5: Don't Panic!

Body Language Bible Rule 6: Keep Practising!

It's normal to look like a reject from *Thunderbirds* at this stage of the exercise. If you look relaxed I'd suspect you're not trying as hard as you could. Remember you're changing something you've been doing nearly all your life. Keep going, though, the work will be worth it, I promise. Your body will suddenly get it and the walk will look great. It won't take ten years, more like ten minutes or maybe a few sessions lasting ten minutes each. Oh, by the way, relax those fingers, they look too rigid!

Learning your Power Pose and your pole positions has been an easy way to create a sound base for all the rest of your body language work. Whatever else you learn as you read this book you should never suffer from neural pruning (dropping something you've learnt to make room when you learn something new) when it comes to these two basic ways of holding yourself. Getting these right is like putting the best petrol in your car or the right food-fuel in your body. Take a few seconds each morning to look in the mirror to get your Power Pose right, then reboot at work when you feel yourself drooping.

Key Points:

- Power Pose – get your alignment right.
- Pole Position – perfect your basic first-step pose for sitting and standing.
- Power Walk – get that Power Pose on the move by perfecting your basic walking techniques.

5

HOW TO DO GESTURES

This chapter will move you from postural awareness and excellence to thinking about all your gestures. Self-analysis can be tough as self-awareness does tend to lead to awkwardness at first. But controlling your body gestures is as vital a competency as being able to control the words that come out of your mouth.

This isn't painting-by-numbers. I'm going to tell you what your non-verbal communications signal to other people, but you shouldn't go running off with the idea that you can compile some sort of photofit bodytalk image of yourself that will be universally loved, admired and respected.

PLAYING BY THE RULES

There are very few rules when it comes to good and bad body language. Although I'm sure there would be something very comforting in creating a special section of body language do's and don'ts, I'm not going to. If I did you'd very quickly start to think I was being unfair. You'd start looking at other speakers and you'd spot at least a few very good orators who used the gestures I'd banned you from using. In fact most of the great speakers I've seen appear to break every 'rule' in the body language book.

Let's have a look at some high-profile names and their effect and image balancing acts:

Prince Charles

We've all read he has a butler put his toothpaste on to his toothbrush for him. This could render him about as popular with the proles as Marie Antoinette. However, his public persona is distinctly lacking in signs of status or even wealth. His clothes look unfashionable and sometimes even well worn and his nervous self-touch rituals and furrowed brow signal anxiety and a touch of subservience.

Ant and Dec

We all know they're hugely successful and therefore very likely to be loaded and living the celebrity lifestyle, but both Ant and Dec have managed to employ a body language technique that their predecessor, Eric Morecambe, excelled at. They have the knack of connecting with the TV camera as though it's a human being. What the viewer sees is two guys looking at you as though they're your friends. You forget about the TV screen and the fact they're in a studio and feel as though they're there in your lounge talking straight to you.

Princess Diana

Being a designer clotheshorse and a princess could have made Diana appear haughty and remote. However she consistently delivered a body language masterclass. She was a consummate mirrorer, flexing her own body language style to fit whoever she was with, effectively lowering her own status and bigging theirs up accordingly. She was also brilliant at producing self-effacing gestures at exactly the right time. On one occasion she appeared at a glittering state banquet looking perhaps her most elegant, with her hair pinned up and a tiara on her head. As she walked away from the cameras she turned quickly and pulled a little face, patting the back of her hair. Like Ant and Dec she was skilled at making her audience feel as though she was their best friend.

Marilyn Monroe

Possibly the best image balancer ever, Marilyn Monroe managed to portray overt sexuality and an almost childlike innocence and vulnerability in equal measures. She did this by alternating swiftly from one to another with each appearing and disappearing at exactly the right speed. One minute she was doe-eyed, with a shy-looking dropped chin. Next minute that chin would be thrown back and her eyes half closed to simulate the state of orgasm. This ability to blend two extremes made her unique. The modern unacceptability of blending these extremes has ensured we won't see her like again, at least not as a popular and universally loved character.

SHOW, DON'T TELL

This is an enduring learning point from this book, so much so that it deserves the rulebook treatment, so:

Body Language Bible Rule 7: Show, Don't Tell

This is a golden rule for all your body language performances.

Words are about *telling* but your body language is all about *showing*. It's a bit like sex. Anybody who *tells* you they are a good lover *isn't*. How do I know? Because they felt the need to tell you. Someone really hot in bed would just let their technique do the talking. When they *tell* you, they're projecting what they want *you* to tell them.

It's the same thing with businesses: 'We're customer-focused', 'We always exceed expectations', 'I'm a people person'; or housemates in *Big Brother*: 'I'm really funny', 'I'm always entertaining', 'I'm a really nice person'. This is all tell, tell, tell. And when they're given the chance to prove their statement? Guess what, they're rubbish.

By showing, you offer proof. You can't tell people you're friendly and warm if your body language is saying 'I'm a sociopath'. However, you could just keep quiet, smile in a friendly way and use open gestures and they'll soon be telling *you* what a nice, decent sort of person you are and how much they want to be your friend.

Showing is a body language thing, then. Your overall signals will take care of the showing. Your hand gestures and eye contact will act as endorsements to your message.

Now: a guide to body language excellence. It's basic but it's easy to do. Any time used will be time invested but I don't expect it to break into your day too much.

A GUIDE TO YOUR OVERALL BODY LANGUAGE SIGNALLING

Let's take a general look at your body language signals and divide them into useful and non-useful 'types'. This is to help you identify different sets of gestures and understand when you're using positive or negative non-verbal communications. Remember, the worst thing is to allow your signals to run along unchallenged.

Physiological Signals

These are all those body signals that you're almost powerless to control, like blushing, blotchy nerve rashes, sweating and shaking or trembling. Although these symptoms have a certain amount of comic value, they're no laughing matter when you're suffering from them.

They are all caused by the power of your mind controlling your body. Although they're all quite natural, they're only supposed to occur in the face of physical danger. They're caused by adrenalin and that rush of energy you get as an animal when you're threatened by a bigger animal. It's your fight/flight mechanism kicking in, but it's your fight/flight response being rather over-zealous, especially if it's triggered by a first date or a meeting with the boss.

Excessive sweating has caused problems for a lot of politicians and TV celebrities. Tony Blair had a famous dose of the wet patches on the shirt during a keynote speech a few years ago and several acres of rainforest went under the axe as newspapers discussed the whys and wherefores of why the PM might be getting so damp. Was it stress? Was it nerves? Perhaps it was nothing more than very hot lights or a warm room.

I've seen hundreds of businesswomen break out in neck blotches when put under pressure. Do businessmen suffer the same problem? Who knows, they're muffled to the beard-line with collars and ties. Perhaps they're gleaming crimson underneath, but the point is you'd never know and that's a key tip for women to remember: if you know you get blotchy on a regular basis then try wearing higher necklines.

Helpful tips

The best way to deal with anxiety symptoms like these is to go to the source of the problem. Stress management techniques will help, but the optimum cure is to work on your inner confidence and your perceptions of external stimuli. Very few scenarios that produce sweating or shaking are life-threatening, they just feel as if they are. Remember that your body is only trying to be helpful; it's the messages from your brain to your body that are causing the problem. I like to call this my 'inner diva', a classic case of the drama queen who over-reacts to any situation in a bid to get maximum attention.

The problem with your inner diva is that once she's kicked off she's self-perpetuating. She starts all the sweating, trembling and blotchiness in motion and then goes off on an even bigger hissy fit about the chaos she's caused to your body. After a few minutes you're sweating about the sweating!

Here are some excellent techniques to shut the diva down.

- Use mental affirmations. One that I teach on stress courses is: 'It's not a lion.' It links to the thought that although your situation might be important it's not a matter of life and death; you're not being pursued by a man-eating lion. Make up your own affirmation and repeat it in your head as a mantra to create calm.

- Breathing exercises will help. Breathe in through your nose until your lungs are at full capacity, then breathe out slowly via your mouth, allowing your body to empty and relax as you do so.
- If your hands get sweaty, carry some freshen-up wipes to cool them before you go into a meeting.
- Never douse your hands or face with cold water in a bid to cool down. The effects will only be transitory as your body will overheat as a result in a bid to balance the sudden temperature change.
- Try cosmetics for blushing or a nerve rash. The ones most commonly available are either a green-tinted moisturiser (both men and women can use this) or a green-tinted foundation or face powder. (Guys might decide to skip these two options.) They don't show as green on the skin, the green tone just negates the redness of the face or neck.
- There are also several products available to remove a sweat sheen from the face. They're also sited on the cosmetic counters but are unisex. They're either fluids or lotions that create a matte finish to the skin.
- Hopefully I don't need to advise the use of anti-perspirant deodorants, but just in case there's someone who has slipped through the net...they will help prevent the curse of the sweat-rings under the armpits.

Performed Signals

These will be the signals that your body produces to get what you feel are your best results from any transaction. Unlike your physiological signals they will be conscious or at least semi-conscious and help define what you feel to be your 'ideal' image state.

Leakage Signals

These are all those fiddles, twiddles, twitches, rituals and other unbidden signals that appear to be your body's way of letting your true feelings be known without your permission. They are the honest brokers of the body language world but they are also a total pain as they are usually responsible for letting truths you'd rather keep suppressed out for all to see.

Micro-Gestures

These are the subtlest of all body language signals and will almost without exception be part of your body language leakage. The good news is that they are so tiny and fleeting that they are often invisible to the naked eye. The bad news is that they can work as subliminal communicators, meaning your audience might not know you did it but they got the message nevertheless.

Compliant Signals

Society depends on compliance. If nobody backed down we'd be extinct within months. Our network of complex dominance and compliance signals is in use on a virtually permanent basis as each transaction we do relies on a harmonious balancing act for it to be successful.

When the balancing act tips, even slightly, our response is far bigger than the event itself.

When you go into a shop to buy goods, you expect to be dominant in that transaction. As the customer you will have the expectation of a degree of compliance from the person who serves you. In fact the word 'serve' gives a huge clue to the nature of the power balance in this situation.

Most shop workers are trained to be compliant, some more than others. Some shops have what they call a 'can do' culture, training their staff to bend over backwards for the customer. Others are less submissive but the balance is always pretty much in favour of the customer.

To signal this compliance the 'server' is expected to smile more as they offer help. But this isn't always the case. Some shop staff excel at raising their own status via body language or behaviour techniques, some of which are so subtle the customer has no idea how they happened or what they did, only that they felt insulted and crushed by what's often called 'attitude'.

In a social group scenario, compliance will be vital for group polarisation. All social groups consist of dominant and compliant roles that can be fixed or transitory. We're all affected by what's called the normative influence – i.e. a desire to be liked and accepted. The easiest way to be liked is to be submissive and compliant. Often mistakenly we feel that doing what other people want will make them like us. Sometimes we discover too late that they have no respect for us.

Status and Power Signals

We all like to flex our power muscles now and again, some of us more than others. Celebrities are possibly the worst Power Posturers in the world, probably because their power depends on a very defined pecking order that is constantly on the move. Power signals aren't all bad then, but it's important you get the balance right.

Imagine going into work each day and having to form a line in order of importance. This is what happens to actors every time they make a movie or TV show. Up there for all the world to see is the cast list in order of status. Not only is the order of names important but so is the size of the typeface used and how long the name is left on screen. This is why we get to see odd-looking billing categories like 'Also Starring' and 'Special Guest Star'. What this usually means is that there's been the mother of all fights between the agent and the production company to hike a star up the pecking order.

In business there are job titles but these have become obscure enough to be virtually meaningless. Hierarchical terms like 'the boss' and 'support staff' are practically extinct.

Money is the biggest pecking order in most companies, which is why earnings are kept strictly under wraps. I once worked with a company where a disgruntled HR manager had 'accidentally' posted a list of everyone's wages to every PC in the firm. The tidal wave of discontent and resentment caused by this has lasted for years and still sluices around to this day.

Status displays and Power Posturing displays are rife in modern life, possibly because of this need to show who's 'the boss'. As I've stated, the dominance/compliance power balance is relentless in our daily lives. As you pick your way through each transaction you show a welter of dominance or compliance signals that you might not even be aware of. Here are some of the categories:

Social power signals

In many ways social power displays are a necessity if a group or a couple are going to form in a way that is harmonious. However, like the normal status signals it's all to do with balance and the blend with comfortable compliance.

Your group of friends will have its own pecking order that is similar to a colony of animals. You might think you're all evenly placed but it would be hugely unlikely that you don't have an unanointed leader for a variety of different scenarios. You might even have one warrior leader and one peace-time leader – i.e.

one person who does all the social arrangements and decisions and one you would all stick to like glue if the group were under physical threat or challenge.

In groups of blokes it's often far easier to spot the main power-broker. Men still use quite obvious Power-Posture signals like splayed legs, puffed chests, fleeting crotch-touch and bum-clench signs and even pit-baring gestures where they sit with their hands behind their heads baring all their delicate body parts to signal how unthreatening they find the person they're speaking to.

With groups of women there are less obvious alpha signs as – in ape terms – women in modern society tend to veer between alpha male and alpha female signals. So the most powerful female could be the one doing the complimenting, hugging or grooming, or she could be the one with the loudest laugh, toughest-looking posture and highest seat or biggest space.

Sexual signals

Like most other gestures, your sexual signals can all have alternative meanings, but nevertheless there are clusters of them that tend to suggest little other than sexual interest or arousal. These can range from mild flirt signals, like smiling, chest-touching (your own!), self-grooming or giggling, to the industrial-strength types like pupil dilation, lip-licking, spine-arching, etc.

Sexual power signals

All sexual couples have a unique power balance and maintaining that balance can be vital for the health and duration of that relationship. A lot depends on the complementary nature of this balance, but even this is more complex than it sounds. Let's say one side has areas of dominance over the other. In this scenario the bloke takes nominal control socially and also dominates around the house, choosing the TV programmes, sorting the finances and doing all the heavy jobs. The female is more compliant except during sex, where she tends to be dominant. She's also very much in charge with the kids.

If this arrangement works it might work on one or both of two levels. It works on a superficial level if both parties perform the roles. This would make it complementary. If they're both happy with those roles then you're looking at sexual power heaven. But then comes a problem. Is one of those parties only performing their role because they want a quiet life? Are they really miscast? Or what if one or both change over time? If the man's only being alpha because he feels it's expected of him or the woman's only acting compliant because it decreases conflict, then either one partner is going to feel suppressed for most of his or her adult life or they're going to split and go elsewhere to find a more desirable 'fit'. Or they might stay in the relationship and have an affair that expresses their true dominance/compliance nature.

The gossip columns are littered with celebrities who split with their partners because the balance of power ceased to work. As threatening as sexual affairs and spells in rehab might be to a celebrity marriage, it's the status imbalance that is usually the deal-breaker.

To look at their photos and TV fly-on-the-wall programmes, Victoria and David Beckham seem to be in a continual state of manageable flux status-wise. When they got engaged it was so obviously Victoria who was the bigger star, with the Spice Girls being mobbed while David walked behind in relative anonymity. Then David turned footie hero and overcame his diffidence in front of the cameras to pose for several key advertising campaigns and fashion spreads. Victoria's career dipped and she was suddenly expected to become a camp follower. Having children probably restored the balance, but whenever there's a lull in the family producing there always seems to be news that Posh wants to reboot her career. Their body language signals seem to have evolved to cope with these huge status fluctuations. While David is always seen in the very traditional alpha role, walking in front with a serious frown and puffed chest while Victoria totters behind him looking fragile, allowing herself to be towed by David as though he's in charge of all the steering and decision-taking, when they're seen working a room it's Posh's very decisive controlling hand gestures around his neck or on his shoulder that place her firmly in the driving seat. This face-saving role-share appears to work for these two.

Madonna and Guy Ritchie have always excelled at the power-balancing poses, although sometimes there have been signs of overcongruence and generally the power signals do seem overall to be tipped in Guy's favour. When he had a movie to plug Madonna would pose in a compliant way, hugging his back or looking adoringly at him to signal he was her hero. When it was Madonna's turn Guy would close down his status signals to big her up, although in her film of her last tour it was interesting to see her confidence as a world-famous diva evaporate visually when Guy was around and we saw a much more compliant-looking side to her. Guy appears to be very alpha-aspirational, keen to set himself up as a real man's man or geezer, and his compliant set-pieces tend to be lacking in enthusiasm at times.

Although their relationships aren't sexual, most TV double-acts depend on well-defined status signals. Ant and Dec, Morecambe and Wise, Cannon and Ball, Del Boy and Rodney

Trotter and even Steptoe and Son made comedy out of the moments of power-shift, although one partner would always be seen as ultimately dominant.

Business power signals

Most offices have two clear leaders: the man or woman with the job title that includes the word 'manager' and the person everyone knows is really in charge. Being a manager is not the same as being a leader. I've met some good managers in business but very few good leaders. Leadership is all about 'being' rather than 'doing' and a key quality of what makes a good leader is charisma.

There are charismatic figures in most large-size colonies. You'll remember them at school and you'll have seen them in the workplace. They're very rarely the boss. Sometimes their job will be borderline mundane but they'll be the ones with the natural status in your workplace group.

These are the colleagues who have alpha power signals. They exude confidence, dominate space and territory and have voice and speech patterns that make people listen when they talk.

Then there are the workers who try to impose their status by active visual displays. Lacking a natural ability to command respect, they Power Posture to the point where they either look ridiculous, like Gareth in *The Office*, or they become hated for being aggressive and bossy.

Throwing your weight around is a risky business, as without a compliant response the Power Posturer will lose face. This will often lead to intensified Power Posturing or a kind of 'do it because I said so' transaction where the only winner will be the one who doesn't have to back down.

HOW TO DO GESTURES

Denial gestures

These come under the heading of shooting yourself in the foot. You make your point but then you take it back by the use of a small mouth-shrug or eye-roll or shoulder-shrug of apology. It's that endearing but oh-so-fatal normative influence at work again, with your desire to be liked over-ruling your desire to have gravitas and make a serious impact.

Denial gestures aren't only prompted by the pressure of a lie, but they do create the impression that everything you've just said was not strictly true. You can try this one at home but only if you have a death wish: next time your partner asks you if you love him or her, say 'yes' but then follow it with a swift eye-roll or shrug.

Metronomic gestures

These are those tapping, time-measuring hand, foot or leg movements that act as your own personal metronome to either speed up or slow down your thinking and bodily movement. As a self-motivator or self-stimulator they're great because they allow you to set your own pace without even thinking about it. When you tap that pen into the palm of your hand the odds are you're trying to egg your brain on to come up with a speedy response or idea. So far, so fab. However, although this is a good tool for self-stimulation it begins to become a bit of a liability when you perform it when someone else is speaking. Your personal metronome will look very much like a 'hurry up' signal to the speaker. This will have two effects:

1 It will make them a much worse communicator. We don't like to be rushed, it makes us crap at anything we're trying to do.

2 It will make you look very rude. Even on a subconscious level.

Autonomic signals

These are mainly stress-promoted gestures that are prompted by all the physiological and intellectual changes that stress wreaks on our bodies. Autonomics include crying, fast breathing, shaking, accelerated blink-rate, etc.

YOUR PERSONAL SCHOOL OF EXCELLENCE

The good thing about body language excellence is that there's no one stopping you achieving it. Oh, sorry, actually there is someone standing directly in your way:

YOU!

When it comes to body language signals you are not only your own worst enemy, you're your *only* enemy. Why? Well, other people want you to be good. They like clear messages that are easy to understand. They're fed up with your horrible habit of scratching your nose as you speak so they're rooting for you like a team of cheerleaders.

You, on the other hand, could be hosting as many as four inner demons who are happily capable of scuppering your communications and non-verbal techniques:

- Your inner heckler
- Your inner animal
- Your inner child
- Your inner diva

Your Inner Heckler

When your gestures work they endorse your message, but gestures can also work against you, turning into your own Personal Hecklers. Why would we want to heckle ourselves? Perhaps the word 'want' is inappropriate! Usually it's something we're driven to do and are unable to stop. These gestures are also called contradictory signals. Ever find yourself telling someone how pleased you are to see them or how interested you are in what they have to say but then find your eyes flicking around the room in what's called an eye shuffle or your fingers fiddling with your cuff or a yawn building as they speak to you? This is your Personal Heckling system at work, shouting out: 'No they're not!' Or have you ever been telling the boss that you're confident and capable enough to get that promotion while your leg starts to shake or your throat suddenly needs clearing several times? This is your Personal Heckler yelling out: 'He's rubbish! Don't promote him, give him the boot!'

Your Inner Animal

We've seen the power of instinctive thought. No matter how much the human animal evolves, there's always that fight/flight urge in all of us and it's usually the first option that presents itself. This means that – under pressure – your body language signals are in conflict. Suppressing all that fear, anger, lust and desire to fight is a daily battle that you think you're winning, but are you sure you've managed to delete every trace of that inner ape? Just check how many times your hands ball into fists when you get mad or you pull your own hair or wave your hands around when you get anxious.

Your Inner Child

Remember those pseudo-infantile re-motivators? As you grow up, your body language follows suit – or does it? We like to think we leave all that thumb-sucking stuff in the pram, but your inner child will surface in your body language every time you're stressed, anxious or missing out on something you wanted. Okay, so you probably don't stick your thumb in your mouth but I expect your self-comfort repertoire contains some form of sucking or chewing, possibly involving the end of a pen or your fingernails. And your face when you're being stroppy is probably not a million miles away from the look you wore as a toddler.

When you get put under pressure or placed in a state of fear or anxiety your sympathetic nervous system and your parasympathetic nervous system get into conflict. The first prompts the fight/flight response and stirs you into action and the second attempts to self-calm. In situations where the threat is more in your mind than in reality, these two battling together will produce some uniquely contrasting body language signals that might look very childlike. Some will be physiological, like blushing one minute and going white the next as your blood drains, and some will be physical, like pacing about before sitting down exhausted. These can also prompt the next response, which I have called...

Your Inner Diva

In charge of all the attention-seeking and emotional set-pieces, shouting, pacing, panicking, going frantic with fear or nerves that are out of proportion to the size of the stimulus, the inner diva is a consummate arm-waver, gesticulating like someone drowning to show intensity of feeling. The pair of you will work happily in tandem to produce a negative own-goal. You feel worried or scared about a meeting, your inner diva eggs you on to fear, anxiety or panic and before you know it you're incapable of measured, calm speech.

Taking Control of Your Inner Demons

- Recognise that your responses to any scenario or transaction can be courtesy of your inner demons. These are all natural, instinctive voices but your leader 'voice' will need to be developed to control all these others to help achieve your own image goals.
- Now's the time to identify that leader voice. It will stand for logic and reason. It will need to be able to take control in any emergency and it will need to be able to self-coach, reminding you of all you stand to gain and everything you could lose if you allow your child/animal/diva voices to take control.
- The name of this voice or state is 'adult'.
- When you feel emotions taking over, focus on this adult state and allow it to steer your body language. Think positively and tell yourself to expect positive outcomes. Let this reflect in your posture and gestures.
- Visualise your adult self. Put a face to it and even a name to it, if it helps. See it coping in an emergency. Then mimic it in your body language. Your adult state is always confident and calm. Repeat this mantra to encourage your body to relax: 'I feel calm, confident and in control.'

It's easy to believe in the power of personality and impulsive behaviour and argue that if you train yourself to respond rather than react to situations and stimulus you're being fake. However you should always remember that your behaviour is not your personality. It's your tool, not your master, and you use it and change it to suit your life circumstances. The human animal survives on its ability to socialise and create strategies. Working on your behaviours is vital, as is being in touch with your 'adult' self. We are all several selves, not just one, and your ability to flex your behaviour via your body language and impact is crucial for your development and success in life.

Key Points:
- Break the 'rules' to get results.
- Show, don't tell.
- Recognise your key states that could scupper your body language. Visualise your adult state and allow that to take over leadership and control instead.

6

A BEGINNER'S GUIDE TO YOUR HAND GESTURES

The next work we're going to do to achieve that control is with your hand movements. We've already created the beginnings of postural excellence and now we need to make sure your hands are what politicians would call 'on-line' with your ideal performed messages. This creates what are called co-verbal gestures, or congruence (as we've already seen in Chapter One).

Your Current Hand Gestures

- What are your self-comfort rituals – i.e. all those fiddles, scratches, stroking, sucking and chewing habits you do when you're under pressure or wanting to self-calm?
- What range of emphatic gestures do you have when you're speaking? Are there some you repeat over and over again? Or do you throw your hands around as you talk?

Be aware that it's easy to 'catch' a hand gesture and not all copy is prompted by inspirational mimicry. Two days after Tony Blair announced he was stepping down from office and Gordon

Brown had stepped up to the plate, the often dour-looking Scot was doing a Blair-style gated hands gesture.

GOOD AND BAD HAND GESTURES

How do you define good and bad gestures? If I asked you to compile a list of each, how many do you think you'd manage? Probably a handful of bad ones and fewer good ones, as it's always easier to know what not to do with your bodytalk than it is to know what *to* do.

But the truth is there are very few gestures that are genuine, dyed-in-the-wool, moustache-wearing, cheroot-chewing bad guys. Many of the 'bad' ones will really come under the 'it depends how and when it's done' category. Like folding your arms. This gesture forms a barrier that can reveal anxiety or aggression. So does that mean I slap an ASBO on arm-folding and ban it from your repertoire? Of course not. I fold my arms a lot. Part of my arm-folding is prompted by a deep-seated shyness but part of it is because I think it looks quite cool. Not all the time, not if someone's engaging me in conversation or offering me a job, but if I'm listening to someone else speak while I'm running a course I use the gesture to let them know they've got the floor. Done at the right time and in the right way, arm-folding is perfectly acceptable.

As is putting a hand in your pocket. As long as you don't fiddle with change, or anything else! One hand in one pocket can look urbane and debonair as long as you strike the right pose to go with it.

Nose-picking could go on your 'bad' list though. In fact I think it would creep right across there without even being told to. And if it did, I'm pretty sure smirking and knuckle-cracking would join it hand in hand.

Let's start with the good guys, though. These are the gestures that ride around on white stallions and call all women 'ma'am'. They rescue kittens from trees and they never leave the toilet seat up.

Good Hand Gestures

Good gestures are either **illustrative** or **emphatic**. Both types of gesture will enhance the effect of your message and the understanding of the listener. I'll also look at **schematic** or **mime** signals and **transfix** gestures.

Illustrative

This means your hands perform a mime to describe the object or action you're talking about. We all know the thumb and little finger gesture that mimes 'call me' when you hold it up to your ear. We also know that if you are describing a child, by placing your hand in the air horizontally, palm down, you're showing the height and indicating the age of that child.

Illustrative gestures aid the understanding of your listener. It's like painting small pictures in the air.

Emphatic

While illustrative gestures show visual pictures, emphatic gestures try to define emotions. We stab, hammer, punch, flutter and wring with our hands to show anger, frustration, concern and anxiety or worry. When you use emphatic gestures you ensure your listener understands your strength of feeling. This is as long as they're congruent. If your gestures play against your message they'll scupper it. For instance, imagine a politician who is canvassing for votes. She says her party will lower income tax to generate wealth for everyone. However when the politician uses the word 'lower' she pushes her hand, palm up, upward into the air. And when she uses the word 'everyone' her hands point towards her own chest. This is where the emphatic gestures fail to do the business.

Tony Blair and Gordon Brown tended to time-share the same emphatic gestures. When they were canvassing votes they'd both use what I call the Matador Stab, pointing both index fingers downward and jabbing them towards the lectern. This emphatic gesture would be too over the top for normal use but as an accompaniment to verbal displays of commitment and 'nailing their point' it worked every time. They also shared a love of a measuring gesture, holding both hands out face-to-face, about ten inches apart, fingers stretched flat. This gesture would be moved around in the air, going to the left (their left) to signal previous problems and to the right to show plans for the future. By employing both hands in the same gesture they appeared to be fully committed to their thought as both their left brain and their right brain were in agreement. It's rare to use an emphatic gesture that employs both hands in sync like this. Usually we tend to gesture more with one hand than the other.

Schematic or mime signals

These are intended to be much more precise and should create deeper understanding of your message. However not everyone speaks the same body language and you should remember that there are cultural variations.

The classic signals do appear to have obvious meanings though. Ask someone how they are and a 'thumbs up' will nearly always signal 'okay'. Hold one hand out and wobble it from side to side and you're letting someone know you're not sure or 'maybe'. Tapping the side of your nose can mean 'keep it to your-self'. However, mime or symbolic signals can be confusing. When Paul Gascoigne famously wept during the World Cup, Gary Lineker looked towards the bench and tapped an index finger towards his eye. I'd always thought he was letting them know there was blubbing occurring on pitch but a quick lip-read seems to suggest he was really saying 'keep an eye on him'.

Transfix gestures

These hand gestures 'park' a thought during a conversation, reminding everyone you intend to return to it. They can be useful markers to signal that there might have been an interruption but the subject matter hasn't been dropped. They can look rude, though, if you use them to ignore the new speaker and suggest you just want them to finish so you can go back to your preferred subject.

The Bad and the Ugly?

Now we've seen what will aid your communication, let's look at some gestural types that can cause problems by disrupting or upstaging your message.

Aggressive hand gestures

We use a lot of aggressive signals during the average day, often without realising it. Most of them will occur as a result of suppressed aggression or frustration but they are visible to the naked eye and will be received as purveyors of ritualised combat or fight intentions.

Aggressive gestures appear when your system goes into a state of aggressive arousal. For most humans there's no follow through or even desire to follow through. A gang of fans going to a football match might well set out for the day with the objective of giving rival fans a good seeing-to but few commuters board the 7.34 to the City checking they've packed their knuckledusters and their can of Mace along with their BlackBerry. Aggressive behaviour in the workplace is just as rife as that at football matches but it tends to be suppressed, masked or displaced. Workers often find that their way of coping with daily frustrations can involve things like slamming down phones, sarcasm, chewing pens or even getting into conflict at home.

Leakage hand gestures

Remember your body language 'leakage', all those give-away signals that act as your Personal Heckling system? Well, much of your leakage will come from your hand gestures, which tend to go out of control once you're put under pressure. Many of your leakage gestures can be misleading, but I've already read you the riot act over 'no sick notes' and that rule has to stand.

Even if your hand-rubbing is down to the chill in the air, if it looks like nerves it will have to stop. If you fiddle with jewellery, take it off for keynote meetings. If you twiddle your hair, tie it back.

Any gesture that's not part of your congruent message will be scuppering your communication via heckling and will therefore have to be deleted from your repertoire. Do this by visualising and then rehearsing those gestures that will enhance your verbal communication.

Self-calm gestures

If this book was about stress management I'd be encouraging you to keep doing your self-calm gestures. They're the sucking, stroking and patting things you do to make yourself feel better when you're under pressure. Unfortunately you do need to ask yourself how many times you'd have 'anxious' on the top of your image projection wish-list.

If you're hooked on self-calms then at least try to develop one that is less visible. If it takes 21–30 days to change a habit, find a new one and make it work. All you need to do is invent a new self-calm gesture, like rubbing the tip of your thumb. Do it for 21 days when you feel calm and comfortable, then begin to use it to calm yourself down when you're stressed. Your brain will learn by association and the new gesture should be subtle enough to keep hidden.

Truncated gestures

These need to go on to the 'gestures to ditch' list. Truncated gestures are the sort you start but somehow forget to finish. Ever watched someone talk who stops halfway into a gesture or mime? These are called truncated gestures. The speaker may pull out a sweet and only get halfway through unwrapping it because they warm to their theme while they're talking, or they start counting on their fingers, intending to count four points off but get lost after one or two, or they raise a finger to make a point then park it because you go on talking. These gestures interrupt the listener. The eye tends to focus on chaos and if your gestures are chaotic in this way they will compete with your words and undoubtedly win.

Truncated gestures are a distraction. Always finish what you've started because your audience will tend to stay where you left them.

Barrier hand gestures

Hands are all too easily accessible when it comes to creating body barriers. You can use them to cover any part of your face or to clutch a wine glass or bag to your chest when you feel under attack at social events. If you're a man, you might even use your hands to perform the classic crotch-cover or fig-leaf pose when you feel under physical or emotional attack. Even a small amount of facial touch will imply either anxiety or even lying, so make strenuous efforts to keep your hands off your face, apart from an index-finger-to-chin touch, which can imply active listening.

Auto-contact gestures

Hey, guess what? Auto-contacts can range from good to ghastly, depending what part of the body you're touching! As the name implies, they are self-touch gestures and will usually imply nervousness or anxiety, but in the case of hair, lip or even leg or arm touch they can also imply sexual interest. So be careful!

Gestural Excellence

So, to sum up: it's easy to spot the gestures that might scupper your communication. These will fall into three key categories:

1 They distract from your message because you are fiddling, twiddling or waving your arms around too much. These are the upstagers and need to fall out of your repertoire. They can also be half-finished, which means they are truncated gestures.

2 They're in conflict with your message. These are all those leakage or denial gestures that heckle you as you speak.

3 They're overcongruent, meaning they're right for the message but so over-the-top or over-repeated that your audience doubts your sincerity.

CHANGING YOUR HAND HABITS

It sounds hideously difficult to change your gestural patterns. For one thing you're probably not even aware of them, and once you are you become too inhibited and self-conscious to look natural. Hands are a bit of a bugger. They're happy to do their own thing when you're not looking but once you start to pay them attention and give them instructions they go into a strop. Often they appear to grow in size and the more you instruct them *not* to do something the more they tend to do it. Try telling yourself not to fiddle with your notes as you talk, for instance. The brain has its own little filter system. It deletes the word 'don't' and only hears the command, so 'don't put your hands in your pockets' becomes 'shove your hands in at the first opportunity and then fiddle with your small change while you're in there'.

Change means sending positive commands, not don'ts.

Remember, it takes 21–30 days to change a habit, which is small fry compared to the benefits you'll be reaping. So here are your easy steps to becoming in control of your hand gestures:

- Be aware of what gestures you're using at present and how you'd like them to change.
- Know your goals. What do you want to do with your hands while you speak? Open, emphatic gestures? Then send that image down to your subconscious.
- Get in front of that mirror again and rehearse, rehearse, rehearse.

Here's a guide to help you through your rehearsals:

- Palms facing up make you look open, honest and compliant; although overdo the palm displays and you could look like a small-time crook or conman. Remember, over-congruent signals are not a nice look. The poker player's rule applies to overacted hand movements – that is, if your opponent displays as though they have a bad hand, expect it to be a good one, and vice versa.

- Palms held to front is a signal to stop or defensiveness under attack. If the palm is flat and fingers stretched it will look like an order. If the palm is more relaxed it will imply you're trying to get someone to lay off.

- Hands balled into fists. If they're down at your sides it will look like suppressed aggression. If they're held at waist height they'll suggest frustration at yourself.

- Hands clasped in front of torso. Held crotch-height they'll look super-defensive as though expectant of a low-blow attack. (By the way, watch out for defensive gestures; when we look as though we're expecting to be attacked we often invite the very thing we dread.) If the hands are loosely clasped waist-height you'll look ready for action and rather confident. If they're clasped any higher you'll look submissive, with the level of submission rising along with the hands. You'll probably stop at the chin and the hands clasped under the chin pose is the most submissive of the lot, fairly inviting other people to wipe their feet all over you. Wringing hands suggest subservient and anxious. A hand-clasp where the palms are pointed at the floor will look juvenile and very much like a pathetic attempt to look cute.

- Hamster Hands is a term I coined for hands clasped nervously high up the body, around chest- or even neck-height.

Doing this will make you look over-anxious to please.

- Hands on hips. This body-bulking gesture can look like Power Posturing. It mimics the first stages of aggressive arousal in animals when they puff themselves up to intimidate their opponents.

- Hands held with tips of fingers joined and palms slightly apart. This is called 'steepling' and it's easy to see why. It normally signals a desire for heightened status, especially if all the fingertips or the tips of the two index fingers point upward towards your own chin. There's a sense of control and precision about this hand gesture that suggests a rather sanctimonious attitude. If the fingertips point forward there's less of the status-posturing, but by pointing all fingers at the other person you'll appear to want them to keep their distance, not because you feel vulnerable but because you feel superior.

- A lowered steeple – when the steepled hands are held around crotch-height or point forwards. This implies critical listening.

- By holding both arms at your sides you'll look odd. This pose will only usually occur in military types or people who have been on presentation skill-training courses. If your arms are held out from your sides like a muscle-bound ape you'll appear to be emphasising your alpha credentials.

- If your hands are clasped behind your back you'll look as though you're keeping them out of trouble. Women who do this gesture can look charmingly whimsical but men will often seem like a frotteur in remission. This last point doesn't apply to concierge staff or shop workers who will use the pose to signal they're ready to serve or help.

- Place one hand in a trouser pocket and you can look debonair and cool, but only if the thumb is still on display. Hooking a thumb or both thumbs into your pockets can look affected in a louche kind of way. Shoving the whole hand in will signal a desire to hide. Ditto both hands, with bells on. Jangling change in your pocket will just look pervy. Avoid jacket pockets at all costs as they're too high to look good, especially when the pockets belong to a double-breasted jacket that is buttoned up. This will look anally retentive (sorry, Your Royal Highness).

- Your hands shouldn't be employed in any business apart from gesturing as you speak. Famous finger-pickers include Frank Skinner and Chris Tarrant, both of whom will perform a full manicure throughout the duration of an interview, which is not a good look.

- Be careful how you employ your index fingers, remember that they constitute a weapon and you could look aggressive or attacking. For example, a finger-baton is when you raise your finger upright and then wave it forwards and back, looking reproachful.

- Rubbing your hands together could imply relish and a desire to get on with the proceedings. Prince William used this gesture en route to his father's wedding. Beware using it when you're in charge, though; it can remind people of a dad at a kids' party.

- When you use your hands, avoid keeping your arms pressed in against your sides. This raises the shoulders and presents like an anxious-looking self-hug. Drop your shoulders as you've learnt to do in your posture exercise and allow your elbows to move out slightly from your waist. (I did say 'slightly'; we're not doing the Birdie Song here!) Get a little air in under your armpits, it will make you look more confident and in control.

- Never allow your fingers to go rigid, stiff and spiky. This is caused by muscle tension and will make your nervousness obvious.

- If you have a habit of re-straightening your tie, buy yourself a tiepin and grow out of the gesture. If you want to be reminded of how this comes across, watch how David Brent did it in *The Office* and how that nervous habit made him look. A tie is a phallic garment worn like a huge arrow pointing towards your willy. Keep touching it and drawing attention to it and...well, you work out what it means.

- Use your illustrative gestures to tell a story. They're useful for fleshing out your words or adding visual pictures to aid understanding.

- Keep your gestures working at about the same pace as your speech, which will make them look co-verbal and therefore part of the same thought processes. Genuine gestures occur just before words as it's easier for the brain to create movement than to formulate language, so to look sincere you should allow your hands to do the talking rather than allowing your words to lead the way.

- Think Fred Astaire. The best movement is in sync so that your entire body looks well choreographed. Avoid anything that looks jerky or uncontrolled. This doesn't mean every movement should look calm, though. You can add impact via added emphasis. But avoid becoming over-choreographed. Super-smoothie movements can make you look false. Think of those politicians who appear to have had every single blink and breath under scrutiny and over-groomed. Pre-Bush, US politicians were too choreographed for UK tastes. No one could accuse Bush over being over-prepared in his Q&A sessions though!

- Open gestures have more impact than closed, but if your arms are spread for too long you'll look like Al Jolson doing jazz hands. Alternate between loosely clasped hands and open gestures.

- Keep gestures in the area from waist-height to shoulder-height. Any lower and you'll look depressed or pervy and higher will imply hysteria or borderline madness.

- Relax your fingers by shaking your hands gently before you meet and speak. Camilla could have been given this advice to overcome nerves before her marriage to Prince Charles, but I spotted her doing it as she approached a group at a reception. Please keep your warm-ups in private. The only invisible work-outs would be gently exhaling to relax your body or the posture corrector, straightening your spine and dropping your shoulders back and down.

- Never use props to keep your hands out of trouble. Although it's tempting to hold a bag, a pen or even some papers you'll find these become an exaggerated version of any self-comfort fiddles. Pens provide such a good insight into your thoughts and emotions that they should come with a government health warning. GBH of the biro is commonplace, and as you twist it, unscrew it, chew it or waggle it you'll be giving away more than you'd choose to.

- Illustrative gestures are grand but make sure you never teeter over the brink and into the world of mime.

Remember S Club 7? Remember how they had a move for every line in the song? I've seen speakers perform very much the same way, miming words as they speak as though talking to the hard of hearing.

When you start to discover your leakage gestures it can cause you to suffer the kind of discomfort that can send you back-pedalling into a state of unawareness. But always remember that ignorance isn't bliss – some work spent studying your leakage signals, then focusing on the do's not the don'ts as a way to edit them won't only rid you of some negatives, it will enhance and add to your body language repertoire as well.

Key Points:

- Study the good hand gestures, like illustrative and emphatic, and work on your bad ones, like the denials and metronomic gestures.
- Make your communications congruent by matching your hand gestures to your words.
- Use techniques like palm displays to imply honesty and avoid gestures like face-touch that could suggest you're lying.

7

HOW TO DO FACIAL EXPRESSIONS

In this chapter you'll be working on your facial expressions and
other subtle give-aways, studying your smile, eye contact and
other facial movements and seeing the effect they can have on
your audience. From your social facial performances to your
screensaver face you'll learn how to project an open, positive
and charismatic image or how to mask when things aren't going
your way and you're feeling under pressure.

YOU AND YOUR
FACIAL EXPRESSIONS

You probably think you're in control of your facial expressions
but the fact is you have very little, if any, idea what your face is
saying throughout the day.

The human face has many more muscles than any other
animal, and they combine to create a complex range of
emotional messages. The urge to create these messages is so
strong we even perform them when we're alone and there's no
one watching.

- What does your smile look like when you're required to perform a social smile – i.e. one that is pleasing or polite, rather than one that is natural and unforced?
- Is your mouth crooked? Does your smile reach your eyes? Do you show teeth or even part your lips?
- What's your normal level of eye contact? How do you behave when you feel under pressure or intimidated?
- Where do your eyes tend to roam to when you're thinking? Do you stare straight ahead or upward?
- Do you ever frown without realising it?
- What does your 'screensaver' face look like? This is the expression you wear when you're not putting your 'best face forward'. Do you look glum or angry?

Your face has three key modes:

1 **Performance**

This is your normal 'going out' face used for meeting, greeting and general chit-chat scenarios.

2 **Masking**

This is the face you apply when trying to suppress negative expressions and replace them with something more polite or appropriate – e.g. masking boredom by feigning interest, etc.

3 **Screensaver**

This is more than just a blank canvas on which the other expressions are painted; your screensaver is the nearest there is to a natural facial expression. You'd likely start in screensaver mode as you prepare yourself for the day ahead. It's the face you pull when you're not pulling a face, although it's a little more complex than that. As we get older our muscles tend to hold memory traces. These will tend to distort your screensaver face, meaning that without any bidding from you it's altogether possible that your screensaver has become a frown or a scowl. It's very rare that a screensaver is anything remotely resembling a smile. I see one woman regularly where I live and her face sports a smile when it's in 'resting' mode. I haven't done a street survey on the effect her expression has on passers-by but I have a strong suspicion that they're mildly troubled by it.

Imagine a camera strapped to the side of your head, filming your facial expressions all day. How much time would you spend performing, masking or in screensaver mode?

Your Social Performance Face

You think your face acts normally when you speak to friends, family and colleagues? Then compare it to the face you wear when you first get out of bed in the morning. The better you know someone the more likely you are to be wearing your normal face when you deal with them, but when you speak to anyone from a friend up to a total stranger the chances are you'll apply your social expression, what psychologists call 'putting your best face forward'.

At work you will be required to use your performance face almost exclusively. Anyone not doing so will usually be deemed negative and moody, especially if they're female. Women in business are expected to smile 80 per cent of the time and most are compliant enough to do so. Hence the way women are often described using that awful word that is intended to be a compliment: bubbly!

If you work in a front-line, customer-facing post you'll probably be required to smile frequently. Otherwise your performed facial expression will probably range between polite, positive, listening, concerned and keen. The higher up you are in the company the less pressure you could have to perform. Sir Alan Sugar wears the rather grumpy face of a man who owns his own business, although Sir Richard Branson is one leading businessman who seems concerned with wearing his high-performance 'smiley' face whenever he's out in public.

There's no dishonour in sporting a social performance face when you're out and about. Your ancestors would have found it a life-saver because scowling and giving other animals the evil eye can get an animal killed.

The changes to your facial expression will create huge changes in the way you are perceived. I'll be talking about love and sex in Chapter Nine, but the 'Look of Love' is one of the most radical changes there is, rendering your face almost unrecognisable by a softening of the features and ensuring your partner will find you doubly attractive and fall in love with you.

Sadly, once you've been through the initial stages of attraction, love and lust your face is likely to return to its 'natural' expression when you're with your partner. In many ways this relaxation of the features can be a relief, because you're in that comfortable zone with them known as 'being yourself'. Trust and comfort allows us to drop the social mask and display our true face to our partner. Unfortunately that 'true' face is rarely the most attractive option. Just as the Look of Love is nature's own Viagra, so this 'true' face might well be nature's own birth-control as it tends to look dour, tired and ugly. Unconditional love is a state we all strive for in our lives, having seen it with our parents and hoped for it with our partners, but it is a rare and unrealistic goal in a relationship that's also founded on sexual attraction. With men and women spending more hours in the workplace than they do at home, what happens when the person at home wears their world-weary face while at work the same person has been trained to wear their 'best face'? I've studied thousands of business people and many of them wear the Look of Love on their faces when they're working because they're a salesperson or wanting to appear charismatic or because they want to suck up to the boss. This leads to a potential blurring of roles that more than accounts for the amount of office-based extramarital affairs.

Dog-Facing

Your route to work will involve a period of screensaver facial expression known as dog-facing. This expression was discovered when prisoners were monitored when the guards were in the room as opposed to when the guards left them alone for a period of time. When the guards were there the prisoners dog-faced, dropping their heads along with all traces of facial expression. This was partly through fear and partly through not wanting to stand out and be noticed. If you commute to work you'll probably dog-face for both of the last reasons. When you sit or stand on a crowded tube you try to remain invisible because drawing attention to yourself in those circumstances can be dangerous. You're in an enclosed environment with many strangers, any number of whom could pose a threat. By engaging in eye contact or attention-seeking behaviour you could risk opening yourself up to approach or even attack. You also place your mind somewhere else and this is reflected in your deadpan expression. Commuting is only bearable if you place your mind in a state of suspended animation!

Interspersed with this intense dog-facing may be moments of high-performance. This would come if you buy a newspaper from a cheerful vendor or have quick chats to coffee-bar staff or security guards or receptionists. This may require massive effort as you've been dog-facing for a long period of time. Often your smile of greeting will only exist in your mind. Ask any receptionist and he or she will tell you that all they see is a stream of miserable faces going past their desk.

Your Emotional Faces

Your key facial expressions are concerned with saving your life. There are primary and secondary emotions. Your basic emotions are those your ancestors would have used in the wild to react to real threats. They include fear, sadness, anger, joy, disgust and surprise. Your secondary emotions are those caused or triggered by your thoughts or imagination. These include love, disappointment, contempt, optimism and guilt or remorse.

Primary emotions have a strong facial response.

Fear or surprise will make you raise your brows, widen your eyes and possibly open your mouth. All these responses will increase your ability to see and think quickly in the face of real threat.

Disgust will prevent you eating food that has gone bad or would poison you. This expression clamps the lips together and twists your mouth, closes your eyes and makes you wrinkle your nose and turn your head away, often from side to side. You might also poke out your tongue to register rejection.

Anger creates a frown that protects your eyes in any potential fight. It also tightens the lips over the teeth, flares the nostrils, puffs out and reddens your face, making you look more terrifying.

These primary emotional responses might be part of your

evolutionary processing, but applied to the wrong situation they can cause conflict rather than saving your life.

'You should have seen the look on your face' is a common comment, but the point is we can't. Unlike your other body language, your only assessments or evaluations of your own facial expressions are likely to be retrospective and even then you'll need to have been filmed or photographed. Snapshots nearly always lie, either because you were putting on your 'happy holiday' smile or because the only unaware shots that were taken got consigned to the bin the moment you clapped eyes on them.

CREATING THE PERFECT FACE

Does the idea of working on your facial expressions make you feel vain or false? Actors have to invent and hone facial expressions all the time and in many ways, and as we've seen in this chapter, we're all actors when we put on a face that will go out and greet the world. In UK culture falseness is one of the worst accusations you can level at anyone. This shows up on a regular basis in the *Big Brother* house where housemates will happily employ all types of bad or anti-social behaviour but insist they're better than other housemates because 'I'm just being myself'. So anyone struggling to sustain the basic life rituals of looking polite, positive and sociable is instantly seen as false and untrustworthy.

The perfect facial expression then should be registering your ideal projected image. However it should also look genuine. Why? Because we fear what we can't understand. One clue to why George W. Bush achieved a second term in office could be because he has what appears to be a very open facial expression. You might not like what he stands for but all those fleeting expressions seem to give total access to his thoughts. We even saw how lousy his masking was when he was whispered the news of the attack on the World Trade Center on 9/11. His face froze as his brain appeared to stall.

Face-Softening

When we see someone or something we like or love two key things happen to our faces. The first is that your features soften, which is why people who fall head-over-heels in love look soppy and there's no hiding their feelings for one another. The second thing is that your pupils will dilate.

Now, there's no way you can make your pupils dilate at will (apart from belladonna, a type of poison, which Victorian ladies used to do to make themselves more attractive), but you can learn to soften your facial features.

There's no point walking into a room full of people who you hope will like you sporting a face that looks like it should be in Madame Tussauds.

To relax your face to create a confident but approachable expression you'll need to do what I call ironing out your features.

- Close your eyes for a second or two and imagine a nice lukewarm iron is running over your entire face, getting rid of all the knotted muscles and frown or stress lines.
- Work it around the eye area until all your facial muscles feel more relaxed.
- Then poke the tip of your tongue into the roof of your mouth to relax any tension in the jaw.
- Then start to apply the smile (the next thing you're going to learn).

Asymmetric Smiling

Emotional facial expressions are – according to many psychologists – controlled by the right side of your brain, which means it's the left side of your face that will seem to smile easiest. Why the left? Well, the right side of the brain tends to operate the opposite side of the body and vice versa.

Take a look in a mirror and try a few facial expressions out. Try faking a smile, too. Often a faked smile is lopsided because one side of the face is able to reproduce an acted smile more readily than the other side.

When we fake it, then, it's often quite obvious to other people. However, faked smiles are so commonplace in society that we're happy to find this fakery an acceptable signal of an appropriate state. Therefore we're happy to see someone smile when they meet us, even though they don't know us. This takes us back to the ape compliant gesture of pulling the lips slightly back from the teeth to create non-fight rapport. We expect a fake smile of greeting from receptionists, waiters, salespeople and even telephone staff who are told to smile when they speak, as a smile can be heard even if it can't be seen.

Like apes, though, we have a horror of the over-stretched smile. This simian sign of aggression is used constantly in business and on social occasions, often by people who are suffering from smile fatigue. Your smile should always look even and relaxed.

To learn a good smile you should always begin with the eyes. The neural machinery involved in creating a genuine smile is different to that used in replicating or faking a smile. The orbicularis muscle of the eyes moves subconsciously in a genuine smile while the zygomatic muscle of the side of the mouth can create a smile voluntarily or involuntarily. Therefore smiling with the mouth but not the eyes will create what looks like a mirthless or joyless smile.

When you study your face in the mirror, cover the lower half with your hand or some paper and try to create a smile using your eyes alone. Soften the eyes as though you've seen a friend. Then imagine you're about to share a joke with that friend. Once you've perfected the eye smile you can go on to work on the mouth.

Start with a closed-lip smile then widen it to a smile that shows upper and lower teeth (although not all of them!). Does your smile look open and genuine or does it look as though someone's shouted 'Say cheese'? Think of something funny if you're struggling. Keep working on your smile until it looks and feels genuine. Remember all the top movie stars like Tom Cruise and Julia Roberts who have perfected their screen smile to the point where it has made them iconic.

Here are some key things to remember:

- Don't hold your teeth edge-to-edge as it suggests stress or tension. This is known as the stretched social smile or the rictus, for obvious reasons.
- Avoid opening your mouth unless executing a natural laugh – otherwise it looks false.
- Never produce what is known as the flash smile or the lightning smile. This is the name for smiles that appear from nowhere and disappear just as suddenly. A genuine smile might appear suddenly but would hang around for longer.
- Also avoid the pinging smile. These are used to devastating effect by celebs but look phoney when employed in real life. This is where your face lights up like a 100-watt bulb but for no obvious reason except to impress.

- Avoid using what appears to be a choreographed smile that bears no relation to the words you're speaking. Margaret Thatcher used this type of smile a lot, smiling on non-smiley words like 'unemployment' or throwing a smile in when she was trying to sound cross.

The Psychology of the Smile – What Your Smile Says About You

THE MIRTHLESS SMILE
Rounded eyes plus a wide, even mouth.
When a smile fails to reach the eyes it looks
false and performed.

THE STRETCHED SOCIAL RICTUS
Very wide mouth, showing upper and lower
teeth. This is an over-stretched social smile,
making you look desperate for approval and to
be seen as polite. It can also look aggressive,
like an animal snarling.

ASYMMETRIC SMILE

This smile is lopsided. Lopsided smiles are common but make your happiness look lacking in genuine warmth, as though you're just trying to make the effort, or being sarcastic.

UPTURNED SMILE

Only the middle of the lips moves up, making the smile look upside-down. This gives the impression of a veneer of sophistication underpinned by misery.

THE MOUTH-SHRUG

A completely upturned smile, with the lips pulled inward. This is often performed upon greeting. It will make you look long-suffering, rather than happy.

HOW TO DO FACIAL EXPRESSIONS

THE PERFECT SMILE
Mouth even, lips pulled back showing upper
and lower teeth, eyes slightly narrowed.
You look genuinely happy.

THE SUPPRESSED SMILE
The eyes wrinkle slightly but the mouth smile
is held in check – you look as though you're
either sharing a joke or trying not to laugh at
someone.

THE TONSIL-FLASHER
Eyes wrinkled, mouth wide open. This
overcongruent smile will make you look like a
parent trying to get a smile from its child. Or it
could make you look insincere. As a bluff, a very
big smile will make you look very very bored.

THE SECRET SMILE
The chin is dipped and the head tilted slightly
to one side. Eyes are raised, lips closed and
lifted lopsided. This is a quasi-flirt expression,
what used to be called a 'come-on'.

ÜBER-FLIRT
Same as above but with one eyebrow raised.

AGGRESSIVE SMILE
Lips pulled right back, teeth bared. In animal
terms this would be a snarl. You'll look deadly.

HOW TO DO FACIAL EXPRESSIONS

LOWER JAW-JUT SMILE
Only the lower teeth are exposed. Pushing out
the lower teeth will give the appearance of
aggression, no matter how much your mouth
tries to smile.

THE CLENCHER
Lips parted but teeth clenched, edge-to-edge.
This smile will look as though you're masking
inner tension or anxiety.

THE SMUG SMILE
Chin tilted upward, lips quite tight, no teeth
showing. Possibly the least popular smile
because it makes you look superior for all the
wrong reasons.

THE KNOW-ALL SMILE
Mouth lopsided, lips closed, one eyebrow
raised. Although this can have some flirt
potential it will mainly make you look as though
you're demeaning the other person.

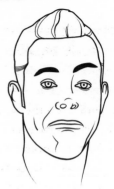

Frowning

It's bad to frown – right? Well, not always. David Beckham has created a signature frown that adds to his image of a sporting hero and he uses it to great effect, even when he's towing Victoria around behind him on a night out. David's frown is an absolute corker because he executes it with one eyebrow. This look can make both men and women go weak at the knees as it intimidates his opponents and implies sexual dominance to women.

A male frown can be a strong sexual turn-on then. Think alpha male and you'll probably be thinking frown. A little touch of anger can do wonders for a guy's image but sadly the same doesn't apply to women. It's almost impossible to find one woman in the media who frowns at all as it flies in the face of the 'bubbly' image that still appears to be 'ideal'. Even female news presenters will either tend to be the bubbly side-kick to the frowning serious male or at the very most present a deadpan expression on screen. If you want to see a saleable frown on a female celebrity you need to look at some moody rock stars or catwalk models who are trying to look aloof rather than approachable.

One of the big problems with frowning is that – if you don't get it right – you can look angry or disapproving rather than focused and sexy.

How to Do Listening and Concerned

Your facial expression is everything when you want to register concerned listening. Tilt your head forward slightly and apply the ghost of a frown. Narrow your eyes very slightly and prepare to do the business with your mouth. From then on it's all down to what's called facial mirroring, which means subtly copying the speaker's own facial expressions or emotions.

Do beware dissonant expressions from your speaker though. This is the term for facial expressions that are directly opposite in sentiment to the speaker's emotions. You see this phenomenon a lot on the TV when someone comes on screen to talk about their own huge personal tragedy or loss. Instead of a sad face they perform a smile and maybe even a small laugh or shrug as though to say 'It was nothing'. This contradictory stuff will usually stem from 'putting on a brave face'. In the UK bravery like this will often achieve a more intense 'pity and comfort' response than sobbing and rending your hair. As a nation, we have a distrust of histrionics.

Eye Contact

Eye contact will make you look confident and in charge of a conversation. However, many training manuals and courses insist you should use it to a degree that I would describe as 'too much'.

By looking away from someone you will appear shy or submissive, but remember what I said about pinning your objectives up before you start to make changes. Is shyness such a bad thing? Think of some people you know who use or used shy body language signals. Four key characters spring to mind: Tony Blair, David Cameron, Princess Diana and her son Prince William. All these people manage or managed to keep on the attractive side of shyness. This means they are able to display terrific confidence in many of their performances yet still keep a high likeability rating because of their use of a dipped head, dipped eyes and bashful-looking smiles.

On the other hand think of those avid fans of the strong, unbroken eye contact signal like Michael Howard, Jeremy Paxman, Jeremy Kyle and Margaret Thatcher, and although you're looking at some strong, controlling characters you're not talking lead contenders in a likeability contest.

You can use your eye contact as a tool of mass destruction then, but you can also tone it down to magnificent effect.

- Use 100 per cent eye contact when you're listening to someone, but add nodding into the repertoire as well or you'll look like a mad staring person.
- When it's you doing the speaking remember to alternate between using eye contact and looking away for short spaces of time. Too much prolonged eye contact when you speak can look intimidating or even dishonest.
- Increase your eye contact when you want to increase your status but use this tool wisely.
- Prolonged bouts of staring only really occur in the real world between lovers who are trying to access one another's minds and/or ASBO louts who are about to punch your lights out. Sadly, intense eye contact will tend to look either passionate or hugely aggressive, which is why the phrase 'Who're you looking at?' is the one that tells you a fight is about to break out.

HOW TO DO FACIAL EXPRESSIONS

Eye Movement

Eye-rolling is often analysed as a natural way to stimulate certain parts of the brain. Unfortunately, though, the direction of the eyes might act as a turn-off to your audience.

- By looking upward and straight ahead you'll probably find it easier to discover your inner script when you're giving a speech or a formal talk, but the advantages of this gesture are completely outweighed by the disadvantages as you'll look pompous or scared or disconnected from your audience.

- Rolling your eyes upward is a straightforward insult to the person you're speaking to as it signals impatience and irritation. The message you're sending is that you're having to look heavenward to ask for patience in dealing with them. It's the visual form of a sigh.

- Your direction of gaze will tend to signal that's where you'd rather be. So if you keep looking at the door when someone's talking, or gazing at other people who walk by, you'll imply you'd rather leave or at least be talking to someone else.

- There are claims that lifting your eyes to either side will suggest either lying or telling the truth. Some psychologists claim there's no proof for this theory but I've studied tapes of famous liars and also monitored people on training courses and I feel that this idea holds water. I'll deal with it at more length in the chapters on reading other people, but keep in mind that if you're being put on the spot and you lift your eyes up and to your left you'll seem to be recalling the truth. However by lifting them up and toward your right you might seem like a liar.

- Glancing away or down at a key point in your dialogue could also make you look dishonest or deceitful. Most people feel their eyes really are the mirrors of their soul and there's a very strong desire to hide them when you're being economical with the truth.

- By keeping your eyes diverted on more of a long-term basis you could look either evasive and shifty or shy. If you drop your gaze when someone looks at you but then raise your eyes to hold their gaze, you could look like a flirt, though!

- An eye-block gesture is when you do a long blink, appearing to signal you want the speaker to shut up.

- Similarly, eye cut-offs occur when you close your eyes for a longer period of time than a blink, usually signalling that you want to remove yourself from the situation or delete what you're seeing or hearing.

- Eye-flashing is that very direct, meaningful look you might throw, usually to your partner when you want to leave a party and he or she has just ordered another drink.

- Eye-puff is when you widen your eyes to register surprise or shock.

- Eye-stutters are when your blink-rate becomes irregular, which will seem to signal confusion.

- The accelerated blink. You'll know when you've been quick-blinked at because it's another signal of irritation or impatience. If someone asks you to do something for them and you really don't want to, it's more assertive to explain your reasons than to agree using a volley of fast blinks. It's a sign that your adrenalin's pumping which is in turn a sign of suppressed anger or irritation. Keep your blink-rate fixed to normal, don't use your body language to drop hints.

- No blinking. Of course it's impossible to stop yourself blinking altogether but I have studied some people who seem to have put their blinks on hold for an extraordinary length of time. Coincidentally they have all been criminals and conmen who seemed to think a wide-eyed gaze would make them look more honest. Not blinking takes a lot of effort and you do need to ask yourself why someone would go to all that trouble unless it was with the intention of deceiving.

Winking

This is a schematic gesture – that is, a more stylised gesture than the mimic gesture – which has been vilified of late by the anti-sexist lobby. I think a lot depends on where you were brought up. In London we use the wink as a matey signal, not a mating signal. It's employed as a tie-sign, which means a way of sending quite complex messages to someone in a simple signal. It's a sign of like-mindedness or a sign of sharing a joke. Sometimes it signals that the winker is just joking about something. As such I think the wink is one of the most attractive gestures in the human repertoire. But then I'm a Londoner. In practical terms it can be seen as sexual harassment in the workplace, which is a real pity.

Key Points:

- Remember, you need to be aware of your facial signals – you're on the wrong side of your eyeballs to monitor them all the time but that doesn't mean they're of low importance.
- Use your facial expression work-outs to create good expressions like happiness, a polite smile and listening or concern.
- Keep your smile in your eyes – this is more important than the smile on your mouth.
- Remember, even the way you blink can affect people's perception of you.

8

HOW TO DO TOUCH

Touch is one of the most significant and powerful body language signals there is. Its power gets lost in the photographs I analyse for magazines and in many ways you do have to experience it for yourself to get the full effect. Even the smallest touch will create a feeling bordering on embarrassment and even distress. Ever sit on a train and find yourself cramped into a small space to avoid accidentally touching the foot of the stranger opposite? Or did you ever go out socially and found yourself blown away when someone lightly touched your arm or your hair while they were talking to you?

Touch is so important we have to set social rules around the use of it. In UK business the only totally acceptable touch is the handshake, but even this gesture can be affected by cultural norms. If a colleague is especially stressed or emotional we might pat them lightly on the shoulder or arm to show support, but anything else could even be construed as sexual harassment.

Social touch might seem more relaxed but there are still strict boundaries, possibly even with a sexual partner.

Just to make life more difficult, touch 'rules' aren't global. There are cultural differences around the world, often with people from warmer climates being slightly more tactile that those from colder climates. In the UK we tend to over-apologise for any unplanned touch and baulk at tapping or patting someone as we chat. Even in our own family environment touch can be self-regulatory. I once worked with three sisters who existed with different touch rules. Two of them were very tactile but they were always more formal with the third, even though their affection was equal.

Most of your touch experience will have been established in your family unit, possibly long before you can remember. New touch is usually created for sex, although you might use levels of tested touch to signal stages of friendship with new friends or business associates.

Even your greeting rituals will be worked on a touch-test basis which is probably subconscious. For instance, you might meet a group of people, only two of whom you have met before and one of whom you're very friendly with. As introductions are made you could perform very formal handshakes with the rest of the group but add a slight squeeze or an extra shake for the person you know. For the person you know well you might use your free hand to add a pat or to use in the shake.

TOUCH-TESTING

Touch-testing means the rituals of touch and check that we use when we start a new relationship. With friends or colleagues it will probably end at the cheek-kiss or hug but with a potential mate it could end with sex.

Successful touch-testing means touching then checking and waiting for the touch to be reciprocated or receiving a signal of approval. To be good at touch-testing, either sexual or social, you need to develop your skills of perception. If you instigate touch, always watch to see the response. Never proceed or go further until you have a green light, either from a smile or a reciprocated touch. One of the worst social or business horrors is the 'tactile' person with no sense of appropriateness, just a desire to get closer!

Tie-Signs

These are signal touches (or glances) that people use to throw non-verbal messages across to one another. The better the people involved know one another the smaller the touch but the bigger the meaning relayed. Long-term couples can transmit massive amounts of information with a small pat, nudge or squeeze of the hand.

Patting

Patting is commonly used as a touch version of 'no' or 'stop'. When people hug, often one will start patting to signal a desire to break.

Patting a child is not the same as patting an adult. What is a signal of affection for one becomes a signal of power with the other and power-patting is used extensively among world leaders to keep one another in their place.

The Forgotten Art of Shaking Hands

A good handshake is vital on formal social occasions as well as in business. In many ways it's like your personal chip and pin, revealing a lot of telling information about you in a very small space of time via the power of touch.

Remember that in simian psychology the sticking out of the hand is a gesture of accepted vulnerability. It's like a signal of submission, used to end conflict and create bonds. An ape will be offering its hand to be bitten off by the dominant ape. You don't need to take things this far, but using your handshake as a signal of power or dominance is clearly barmy. It's performed to introduce less conflict and more rapport.

Do you give good shake? Most people think they do, but most people also think others' handshakes are often lousy. This contradiction suggests we're not as good as we think. It's rare for anyone to be taught to shake yet it's such a vital form of communication and you'll fall at the first hurdle if your shake is a shocker. Here's how to shake hands well:

- Who shakes hands in business? Everyone, apart from those with cultural differences. This isn't only a sport for men. I still meet business people who suspect it might be a guy thing, though.
- Who extends their hand first in business or social greetings? The host. Period. It matters not who is higher or lower status. If you're a gofer greeting God you still put your hand out first.
- To create seamless shaking choreography always extend your hand from a distance of about six feet. This is what's called an intentional gesture and warns the other person what's coming.
- When you walk into a room or office always make sure your bag or anything else you're carrying is in your left hand so your right is free to shake with. Transferring paperwork and mobiles at the last minute is not a good look and lets everyone know you weren't expecting to get a greeting.
- Use names and introductions as you shake, plus eye contact and a smile.

- Keep the hands just below waist level as you shake.
- Make sure your own hand is dry and cool. If you suffer with sweaty hands use freshen-up wipes in the loo before you make your entrance.
- Never be seen wiping your hand before you offer it. This looks disgusting.
- Or after you've shaken, which implies you want to remove all traces of the other person's hand from your own, signalling revulsion.
- Palm must touch against palm. Offering just your fingers is foul. Put your hand out in the vertical position. Extending it horizontally is a relic from the past that comes under the heading 'power-pumping'. Getting your hand on top in the shake doesn't make you alpha, it makes you a nerd.
- Shake up and down about three times.

Remember, handshaking is about the only form of touch permissible in business, so make the most of it by showing enthusiasm. Never back away as you shake or offer a limp hand that feels like a dead fish.

However, avoid the cruncher, too. Think firm but not crushing. Apathy shows weakness but over-enthusiasm can be just as bad if it includes the use of pain to make your point.

Greeting rituals are full of hidden meaning. Any added touch, patting or prolonged shaking will all register subliminal signals about closeness, enmity, status, etc. In the UK it's unusual to add any extra touch but it is becoming more popular. I watched Prince William going down the line of teams during one FA cup final and it was noteworthy that he changed his style of handshake several times. This is borrowing from the US and – like most American greeting rituals – it only works if it appears spontaneous and sincere. Shaking and adding an arm-pat below elbow level will register you're extra pleased to see the other person. Patting above elbow level creeps into the power-pat remit, looking like a friendly attempt to register control. Higher pats will signal a more obvious show of the same. Grabbing the one hand in two of your own is known as the Hand Sandwich. This is also ultra-pally on the surface but it renders the victim helpless by trapping him or her so it can have sinister overtones. It must seem spontaneous otherwise it will appear cheesy in the extreme. It's also useful to vary your shake in a group where you have mixed experience. I was recently introduced to some strangers at work, but in the group was one guy I knew slightly and one I knew very well. To offer the same rather formal shake all round would have looked odd so I added an extra squeeze or arm-touch to the two I already knew.

Bowing

Do you bow? You probably think not. Bowing sounds über-formal and rather outdated, the kind of thing you'd be asked to do if you were introduced to a royal. Bowing is a very important facet of Asian greetings, with the amount and depth of the bow signifying status and importance. I bet you also bow on a regular basis, but without realising it.

When we meet and greet there's often a tendency to offer a mini-bow, that is, a slight dipping of the head or leaning forward to diminish height. Where the bow is exaggerated it will register strong compliance, especially if the face is lowered, but often it will be performed in an attempt to look charming. In business the bow can also look cynical. Women are often

shorter than guys, and by dipping their height as they're introduced, men can emphasise the woman's lack of inches while still
managing to look gallant. However, it's probably better not to.
A more obvious version of the bow intended as gallantry would
be the back-of-hand kiss. While he was in office President
Chirac was a serial hand-kisser but the gesture always teetered
between charming and chauvinist. It was horrible to watch
female heads of state forced to blush prettily as he did it. He
famously missed out Margaret Beckett once and it had to make
you wonder why.

Hugging

Hugging is a UK social staple, and as British business gets more
touchy-feely, nervously pushing the boundaries slowly further
than the safety of the traditional handshake, so the greeting hug
has become a common ritual of bonding and friendship. In
many ways this gesture is an anomaly. The torso closeness is a
gesture we'd normally associate with the tightest of physical or
emotional bonds and yet it's almost more common between
vague-ish business acquaintances than it is with social friends,
lovers and relatives.

The business hug is all about power, not affection, although
it is dual-purpose, making the huggers look amiable at the same
time. Think of other physical sports like wrestling and you'll get
a clearer idea of the point of the hug. This is generally a male
thing although businesswomen have been known to indulge.
Women are often mindful of breasts though and so tend to place
a hand on one another's shoulders to avoid bosom contact. Men
work in the opposite way: the chests are crushed together but
the genitals kept as far apart as possible.

Men also have ways of emphasising their heterosexuality

while performing what could be seen as a sexual gesture. By patting one another on the back, often quite brutally, they show off their testosterone in case anyone should get the 'wrong' idea. The pat or back-slap has another very basic function: it's a signal to break the hold. Whoever pats first can therefore be seen to be either dominant or reluctant.

The Air-Kiss

This once rather arch and camp greeting ritual has now entered mainstream business society and is used extensively, not just by women. There's a jolly sense of irony about the gesture that means it will often be mocked even as it's being performed. This mockery is evident in the mutual laughter and exaggerated 'mwa mwa' noises that mimic the act of kissing.

Why the joviality? To an outsider this has to be one hell of a complex ritual but to those in the know it's quite simple. Straightforward cheek-kissing can be very sweet, but the over-done type is making a shared joke of the whole process. It's taking the mickey out of the Baroque-ness of it all.

Air-kissing comes with no set of etiquette rules regarding how many kisses and which cheek to go for, so it's up to you to take control. Place your hands lightly upon your visitor's shoulders to steer them. Go your right cheek to theirs first, then go for the other side. Then end.

Power-Patting

These are small signals we send to one another via touch or possibly glance that – despite their apparently fleeting and innocuous nature – are full of meaning.

Did you ever get patted by your mum or your partner?

How about that moment when you're just agreeing to that fourth glass of wine at a party or launching into that very long joke? You receive a gentle arm-touch to start with which is a kind of amber warning light. Then follows the two swift, sharp pats or taps which have a much more sinister meaning. What do those taps mean? Divorce. Soon. If you don't shut up and get me home.

Being patted as a child was different. In those days it registered approval or parental pride. As an adult in business, though, getting patted is a whole different ball game. A once-friendly gesture from your parents is a much different thing when you're working as it places the patter into the higher-status role, where they feel it's their right to offer approval for something you've said or done. Patting during a greeting ritual is riddled with silent and subtle signals. Ignorance is no excuse, so here's a swift guide to the messages you'll be sending out:

- Hand-patting: only for hospital visits.
- Wrist to elbow arm-patting: suggests the person you're greeting is elderly or frail.
- Elbow- to shoulder-patting – macho and matey, jovial, implies you have an extra-curricular shared interest like playing golf.
- Shoulder-patting on the side of the shoulder – much more of a physical attack, like trying to disarm your enemy.
- Top of shoulder patting – a physical attempt to hold your visitor down or restrain him or her. A blatant attempt to raise your status while lowering theirs.
- Back-patting – über-parental and therefore a put-down. Implies the visitor is in need of your approval.

- Head- or cheek-patting – only try this one if you're into martial arts. This implies your visitor is severely mentally damaged. Or it will signal you're having an affair.
- Bum-patting – don't even think about it.

How Not to Leak

Giving a good greeting isn't the hardest thing to do in terms of choreography, but emotionally it's more challenging than you think. It's unnatural for animals to go padding off to perform affectionate or passive rituals with other, strange animals. If they did they'd be dogmeat. So your leakage – that is, body language that gives away what you're really thinking – is likely to involve signals of fear, which in turn will emerge as embarrassment. Your denial signs are likely to include:

- **Looking away as you kiss, hug or greet**

  This is called distracted kissing and it looks terrible. Always give the person you're greeting your undivided attention, even if it's only for a short space of time. Looking around signals you've got other, more important people in your sights.

- **Dithering**

  This is the kiss of death to your charisma rating. Put simply, charismatics don't do dithering. Once you dither during a greeting you're dead in the water. You'll put your hand up then drop it and they'll do the same and then you'll both be waving out-of-sync, floppy arms at one another for the next century or so. Or you'll go for that third air-kiss and they'll back away or you'll clunk noses. Go for your greeting with confidence and be definite about how it's going to look.

- **Giggling**

  This can be prompted by nerves but it creates paranoia, so try to suppress it if possible.

- **Leaping away after your greeting**

  Jumping like a scalded cat or even doing a little hand-wipe after shaking will also signal rejection. And hold that eye contact for a second after you greet to make it look as though you're genuinely interested in the other person.

- **Bringing your hands up as a semi-barrier**

  This is like a knee-jerk defence signal after the openness of your greeting. Avoid any barrier gestures after you've finished your ritual. It's easy to fold arms, crotch-cover, raise a glass higher up your torso or clutch at your bag after doing a greeting.

- **Careering**

  This has nothing to do with job-enhancement, I mean careering as in rushing off clumsily after you greet someone. It's a classic mistake, but it causes disaster. You do your greetings, your brain goes into embarrassment over-drive, you go to walk your visitor to the lift and you forget to take note of your surroundings, crashing into another employee or the reception coffee table or a chair. From there it's downhill all the way. Move off with dignity, don't rush, leap or do a mid-air leap, twist and twizzle.

Meetings and greetings need to be polished performances if you're going to avoid the clunky, clumsy stuff that usually occurs during introductions. It's good that there is very little in the way of set etiquette rules but this can also lead to body language disasters. I often wonder why we pay so little thought to simple rituals like the handshake when it's so high-impact in terms of instant perceptions. Working on your signals will give you an instant and easy advantage, both in business and at social events.

Key Points:

- Touch is a powerful affector – even subtle touch will need conscious thought and maybe preparation.
- Touch-test whenever possible. Was your touch accepted? Did the other person signal for you to proceed or back off?
- Work on your greeting touch, like handshakes, hugs and air-kisses. These rituals create an important first impression – get them wrong and you scupper your initial impact.
- Greeting rituals can go wrong if you lack confidence in your approach. Getting your own personal choreography right is important if you don't want to end up careering or dithering.

PART THREE: USING BODY LANGUAGE IN THE REAL WORLD

Although most people recognise the importance of body language during meeting and flirting processes it's easy to underestimate its impact on every aspect of our social lives. When we leave work for the day we often rush to get home so that we can drop the 'mask' and truly be ourselves. But that constant lack of masking can mean we forget to create body language cues that will help us avoid conflict or relationship breakdown. This part of the book examines some of the pressures of meeting people, dating and mating, and gives advice and tips to encourage long-term success in all your relationships.

9

HOW TO DATE AND MATE

This chapter focuses on meeting, dating and mating. It explains how you first signal attraction and why you're attractive to other people. It will also help you build rapport quickly and help you make yourself more desirable to someone you fancy.

THE PROCESS OF ATTRACTION

What attracts us to a mate? How long have you got? There's a strange irony to the attraction process that humans somehow fail to get, which is that the factors that we use to define an attractive person are often the factors that guarantee someone will be *unlucky* rather than lucky when it comes to meeting a mate and sustaining a relationship.

Open any magazine or newspaper and you will see pages of 'beautiful' people who fit the perceived criteria for beauty and perfect looks. Almost without exception the women will be slim, even just after childbirth, large-breasted, and have symmetric, perfect features and an unlined, almost expressionless face.

Any female celebrity is expected to maintain her slim body and unlined face throughout the ageing process, to signal youth and breeding ability. Women in their forties, fifties, sixties and seventies will be expected to avoid 'letting themselves go' by using cosmetic surgery to replicate the ideal image, which is something between childhood and adolescence. Models, who don't have to have the acting or performing talent that tends to come with age and experience and can therefore fit this 'ideal' profile of beauty, will be roughly between the ages of 14 and 19.

So what's wrong with clear, unlined skin and a toned body? Nothing if it's natural or at least natural-looking. An image of youth is an image of breeding potential, and – in evolutionary terms – it's natural for a male to opt for a female who appears to have many breeding years in front of her.

It is a fact of celebrity life though that the most 'beautiful' or most 'perfect-looking' women, the ones we set up as ideal and whose looks we spend money trying to emulate, are rarely lucky in love or comfortable living alone. Most fall into some hideous dark emotional pit of dating and being dumped, dating and being dumped.

Now look at women who do seem to find success in their relationships. Often they're less than perfect on the celebrity Richter scale of good looks. There is a huge discrepancy between the women men claim to fancy and the women men really like. Women that men really like have an added X factor when it comes to signals of attraction. That X factor is called body language. Here's why Barbie-doll perfection can actually repel rather than attract:

- One of the greatest signallers of attraction is the face. In its normal state the face relays masses of information to a potential mate, most of it extremely subtle. Youthful beauty is often deadpan because personality is less of an issue and breeding potential more important. As a woman gets out of her teens it will be her facial expressions that have resonance for a male. He will be extremely attracted to and turned on by facial movement rather than facial features.

- When we fall in love, nature creates a facial expression that I call the 'Look of Love'. Burt Bacharach wrote a song around it. It's a dramatic change of facial features that occurs when you look at the object of your affection and desire. Your eyes soften, your facial expression softens, you acquire what can only be described as a soppy smile and everyone around you knows you've fallen in love.

- You also use your face to signal tie-signs. These are all those small, subtle glances, nods, eyebrow-raises and pursings of the lips that any close couple will use to communicate. They don't need words; these tie-signs will speak volumes.

So where does a deadpan facial expression fit into this love portfolio? The kind of expressionless face sported by models and some actresses and the kind of facial deadpanning created by Botox is – in romance terms – a signal of being emotionally cut off. For most kids it's the face their mother uses to let them know she's really, really, scarily annoyed. It says, 'I have no feelings for you any more.' It's the face that any husband or wife will know signals the absolute end of a marriage. So lifted, Botoxed, unlined, expressionless faces become part of our Personal Heckling system, signalling 'go away' (or worse!) to the bloke we're trying to attract by somehow prolonging our youth.

Big breasts on a skinny body might appear to be a man's idea of heaven. Many men read porn and 90 per cent of porn features girls who are as skinny as whippets but sporting massive great jugs. This look is seen by many men as their social ideal – i.e. the one body shape they can all share a drool over. Men like to keep a tight group allegiance. To this end they need to be seen to admire the same woman. For men it's all about status. The alpha male in a group has to be the one who can pull the best-looking girls, therefore the profile of what's 'best-looking' needs to be created by consensus and more 'deviant' tastes suppressed.

In animal terms the sexiest parts of the female body are the bottom and the vulva. Because humans opted to walk on two legs, thereby hiding both from view, the obsession with breasts and lips began, with rounded breasts and cleavage mimicking the bottom and painted, reddened, pouting lips mimicking the vulva. Ironically women who boost their breasts with silicone, uplift bras and 'chicken fillets' are often the same women who also diet to get rid of their bums, therefore luring blokes towards something that no longer exists. It's only thanks to celebrities like Jennifer Lopez and Beyoncé that the female bottom has had something of a recent revival.

Body movement is one of the great creators of sexual and romantic attraction. We're attracted to people for many complex psychological reasons, not just because they look like a Barbie/Ken doll and our friends would approve. Your sexual programming is something even you would be hard-pressed to understand, which is why our life mate is rarely someone who could be described as universally attractive. When we see a potential mate we also see echoes from childhood and patterns of behaviour plus the visual signals that our subconscious locks into, and the attraction is made. If we only date people we think our friends would approve of we're likely to make some very poor long-term choices.

Men will also be placed under pressure to depict the social ideal image of attraction, but in many ways they're luckier. In a male, attraction is also linked to power. An alpha ape is also the sleekest and best-looking ape in a colony but in human terms the looks factor isn't always necessary if the guy has money and/or high status. Or even if he has good 'fight' potential, which just means he looks like the strongest male in the group. These signals are linked to a time way back in our evolution when the female needed protection while she produced the babies. Male celebrities are likely to be luckier in love than females because their range of 'ideal' options when it comes to good looks attraction is far wider. Would a female version of James Gandolfini (star of *The Sopranos* and no matinee idol in the looks department) have a strong male following? And yet he regularly appears in polls of the sexiest men onscreen.

Flirt signals are a common sight on the celebrity landscape and most leading celebs use them to raise their profile and public desirability by flirting into the camera at key occasions. Often they'll even use a handy partner to 'flirt off'; they will smooch and cuddle the partner but turn their eyes to the camera at the same time. The message from this type of flirting is clear: it's all part of a public desirability process that has little connection with or concern for the long-suffering partner. If there's no handy member of the opposite sex available, celebrities will happily employ same-sex flirt signals or even smooch up to small pets, like Paris Hilton with her dogs.

Genuine Attraction Signals – How to Give Them and How to Receive Them

I'm often asked about the best way to attract a mate or flirt. Sex sells, and so there's a whole raft of books on the subject;

however, most of them tend to bark up the wrong tree. Active flirt signals, the kind of stuff you'd need to read about before launching yourself on to an unsuspecting potential mate, do tend to be a little overly dramatic and often veer into what I can only describe as retro-camp, with fluttering eyelashes, self-touch that would have your mates yelling at you to 'get a room' and hair-flicking that would send most hair extensions flying off into space.

Forget all the fifties movie star stuff then and concentrate on the subtleties of animal attraction. Most of your genuine signals of attraction will happen instinctively and you probably won't be aware of them, for instance:

Pupil dilation

When you see someone you like your pupils will dilate. This state of dilation will also make you more attractive to the object of your desire – in tests using sets of identical twins, the one with the dilated pupils was always the one picked out as being more attractive.

Breathing

Once you get into a state of initial arousal your breathing will become marginally more shallow and rapid. This breathy look was perfected by the most famous sex idol of the twentieth century, Marilyn Monroe.

Voice

Another effect of this breathy approach is to lower your vocal tone. A slightly husky voice is always deemed sexier in both men and women. Genuine sexual arousal will cause this naturally.

Arching of spine

The spine will become slightly more arched in both men and women. This raises the chest and makes it look more predominant, offering a view of bottom-mimicry in women and emphasising alpha strength in men. In women the spine will often arch into an S shape. Kylie Minogue exaggerates this body shape when she appears on stage. It has the double advantage of making both the breasts and the buttocks more prominent.

Mate and breed rituals

In men this will mean puffing out the chest and splaying the legs, and in women it's all about hair-tossing and smiling. When we fancy someone it's hard to suppress a smile. In animal terms this teeth-baring does more than just register empathy and a lack of desire to fight, it also shows off the teeth, which can register good health or poor-quality breeding stock. No wonder cosmetic dentists offering teeth straightening and whitening are so popular!

Blushing

Sexual attraction will often produce blushing. This can feel like hell if you're the one with a face like a furnace but it can make you more attractive to your potential mate. Blushing signals shyness, which in turn suggests virtue and innocence, but at the same time it also mimics the facial flush that occurs during orgasm. Get out the blusher!

Eye buzz

When you see someone you find attractive your instinctive desire will be to gaze and appraise. This prolonged, first-glance eye contact is one of the strongest flirt signals in your repertoire. By extending your gaze for one second over the normal time you'll be telling your potential mate a lot of very complex information to do with sex and romance. Modern manners tell us it's rude to stare so you'll probably alternate a prolonged gaze with a dropping of the head and the eyes, followed by the secondary glance upward at the other person. This second glance will confirm your interest in him or her as a sexual partner.

Grooming gestures

Seeing someone you find attractive will remind your subconscious that you need to present yourself in the best light. This means self-grooming rituals including hair-touching and checking gestures.

All of these rituals will not only let your potential mate know you're interested, they will also develop his or her interest in you and make both of you appear more attractive to one another at the same time. The phrase 'their eyes met across a crowded room' does hold true in current life, as does the concept of love at first sight.

How to tell if he fancies you

- Eye-gaze is the first step. He'll catch your glance and hold it for a half-second longer than normal. Then he'll look away. Then he'll look back.
- He should then change his state in some way, either succumbing to shyness signals like dipping his head, blushing or pulling in his lips or having an accelerated pace of movement, sometimes getting jerky or clumsy.
- If he's with his mates they'll all notice his changed state and will all look over to check you out.

- They'll then probably start mock-hitting him to ridicule him. This is a strange male-bonding ritual that is intended to remind him that male friendships are more important than girls and sex.

- Nature will urge him to perform 'chest-banging' rituals to show off his alpha and sexual credentials. The first change will be a slight puffing of his chest, then a splaying of the legs. If he's in a confined space or crowd he might also perform pelvic jiggling or small bum-thrusts to show what he looks like when he's having sex. (I have to point out these are subconscious responses and very subtle. Any man who starts dry-humping the bar when he sees you should be given a very wide berth!)

- Another form of chest-banging is showing off. This will be rituals like punching his mates playfully or even wrestling them, throwing peanuts into the air and catching them in his mouth, laughing loudly or drinking too much.

- If he comes across to talk you should begin to see signs of face-softening. His behaviour and facial expression when he speaks to you should be different from the way he looks and speaks to everyone else in your group. The urge to smile will intensify with time. Men usually attempt to suppress these smiles, so expect to see a struggle going on with the mouth.

- He'll feel a deep desire to check your body out once he's established his eye-buzz credentials. A top-to-toe sweep is a give-away.

- His next job is to single you out and separate you from the group. He'll gradually get closer and begin to stand in a position that starts to cut you off from the room, so that he gets your undivided attention.

- Don't expect early touch but do expect intentional touching. This is a public signal involving placing an arm on the bar behind your back or your chair, not touching but mimicking a hug.

- Or he might get playful, doing joke-hitting. This is part of the sexual touch exploration ritual. It is really only appropriate once you start to get to know one another. Anyone who uses play-hits as a chat-up should be avoided.

How to tell if she fancies you

- The eye-buzz is the same for both sexes – expect that first gaze to be held marginally longer than normal.

- She will then look away in a downward direction, pause, then look back at you. This is a shyness display that once would have signified virginity.

- She will face-soften, possibly smiling although possibly not right in your direction.

- Most girls will do a quick grooming audit, touching their hair or clothing quickly.

- Postural echo can occur at this stage. You might find you're both moving in a synchronised way.

- She might also try a more extreme form of mating call, like laughing extremely loudly or flicking her hair all over the place.

- Watch for the slight arching of the spine as she holds herself upright.

- When you talk, expect increased eye-gaze plus some lip-licking.

- Girls are very good at marking their territory to signal to the other girls that a guy's taken. This will involve some very fleeting form of touch, possibly on the arm or shoulder. If she picks a thread or speck off your top she's being intensely possessive.

- Tapping or patting your arm or leg might increase if she thinks she's not getting enough of a response.

How to tell if they're not interested

- They turn away after the first glance.
- Their facial expression doesn't change.
- They create more barriers, either folding their arms or raising their wine glass to chest or chin height.
- Their eyes continue to scan the room while you're talking to them.
- Their eye-gaze moves towards the door in an intentional gesture.
- They begin to face-touch, signalling anxiety or boredom.
- Their smile begins to look stretched and fake.
- Their torso turns away from your direction.
- The classic wisdom is that she'll cross her legs away from you if she's not interested. This isn't always accurate though. Girls re-cross their legs to be comfortable. Also, if you're sitting side by side, crossing her legs away could mean her pelvis moves closer to you.
- Ditto with the direction his or her toes are pointing. This isn't exactly a 'take it with a pinch of salt' theory but eye-gaze is a better indicator of interest.

How to Flirt

When your eyes connect, then, you register the first stages of attraction. Once you get into conversation, the eyes will still be the main affectors.

One of the best forms of flirting is to use active listening signals. There's no huge sex display involved but it does begin the ritual of sealing you off from other people and creating a sense of being a couple.

The techniques are easy as they're very similar to non-sexual listening signals, with one extra and very important point. Use eye-gaze as you listen and combine it with all the nodding and mirroring we've discussed in earlier chapters, but add one more dramatic eye gesture: once you've held the eye-gaze for a certain amount of time, allow your eyes to drop down to the speaker's lips for a second or two. Soften your facial expression. This will register genuine attraction and a desire to kiss.

When you first pair off, your eye-gaze will be tentative. As you fall in love and lust it intensifies to the point where it almost looks obsessive. You'll sit in pubs, clubs and restaurants gazing into each other's eyes in an attempt to plumb the depths of his or her brain.

As the relationship becomes stable your gaze will direct outwards more, letting other people know you're an established couple and accepting visitors again. You'll still eye-check as you speak, though, often inviting your partner to join you in the conversation or checking his or her reactions constantly. This defines a state of couple dependency. It can be hugely annoying for friends, who wonder why the confident person they knew is suddenly having to refer back to their partner constantly with checking phrases like 'We did, didn't we?'

Sadly, as a relationship goes long-term, so eye-gaze and face-watching decreases, often to a point where it barely exists at all. This is the point where you know your partner as well as you know yourself and so stop checking for changes. This is also known as the point where you take him or her for granted.

It can often get to the stage where one may say to someone outside the relationship, 'My partner doesn't understand me.'

Eye-gaze is vital for a healthy and happy long-term relationship. It's a performed part of the workplace culture, so imagine the impact of being face-watched at work, which is like a stroke to the ego, then not watched at home, which feels like being ignored.

Watching and looking at your partner is also sexually stimulating for men and women. You fell in love and lust with what you saw. When you stop looking you stop doing foreplay.

First-Stage Touch

I've mentioned the powerful technique of touch-testing in the previous chapter. Although this technique applies to life in general, it will be a vital step in your mating rituals, too.

Touch-testing means working from social to sexual touch in stages and checking at each stage to see if it's accepted and reciprocated. This is a natural process during meeting, dating and mating, but just because it should be a 'natural' ritual doesn't mean it's easy to do.

Think of all your first touch encounters as exploration. There's the standing joke where a young guy sits in a cinema on a first date and pretends to yawn and stretch so that he can place an arm around the girl's shoulders. He then has to keep that arm on the back of the seat until he can pluck up courage to place it on her body.

Although this scene might make you laugh, it should also sound familiar. Apart from the earliest days of a sexual/love relationship, where almost no touch is taboo and sexual approach is welcomed at any time, all touch works on a traffic light system.

THE BODY LANGUAGE BIBLE

- Touch-test your way from the first stages of touch. Be tuned in to your potential partner's responses. Look for a genuine smile or reciprocal touch. If he or she stops moving or becomes overcongruent – for example, giggling – you need to take it as a potential red light. It can be a sign of embarrassment.

- Start with social touch first. If your partner isn't interested he or she will find it easier to turn you down and you won't lose face.

- Social touch during a conversation (not to be used on total strangers, but proceed with an amber light once you've got into a sociable and mutually acceptable conversation!) can include a light touch on the hand, arm or back.

- Steering touch can signal the first tie-signs. This would mean touching their elbow to steer through a crowd, or placing your arm behind their back for the same purpose.

- Loud music in a club can induce more intimate social touch than would be acceptable anywhere else. It means even very first meetings can include facial proximity as you yell in one another's ears, plus shoulder or even torso touch.

- Dancing is a ritual that was often used to create quite intimate stages of touch but in a formal way. Ballroom existed in an era when stranger touch would have been very restricted and even kissing might have taken several dates to achieve. Dances like the waltz or foxtrot involved the possibility of torso-touch, but to keep it all above board the hands are employed in a very formal manner.

- Dance rituals have strong links to animal mating rituals. Modern dance is more about sexual display than touch as couples tend to dance apart, but there are still several gestures of touch-intention, where touch is mimed, or some moments of touch followed by separation, mimicking the touch-test rituals of sexual approach.

- The second stages of sexual touch involve what are still subtle displays, although the effect and intentional signalling is more intense. These touches include fleeting face-touch ('You have an eyelash on your cheek'), wrist or inner arm touch ('Can I smell your scent?'), or more prolonged hand touch, usually accompanied by more intense bouts of eye-gaze.

- Stage three will often involve 'ownership' rituals. This is where someone (often the female) begins to mark her territory by using touch to let other females know the man she's with is taken. This usually means grooming touch, smoothing a collar, for example, or picking a hair off his jacket.

- Stage four will move into exclusive touch, the kind of touch that has no going back as you can't pretend it was anything other than a sexual advance, like thigh touch, mouth touch or more prolonged torso-touch.

Instant Attraction

To create the belief that we've fallen in love in an instant of first meeting, nature also makes us perform two more subconscious rituals that can be effectively aped in a more conscious manner.

- **Torso alignment**
  To create a feel of instant karma, get your body facing his or hers front-on, even across that crowded room.
- **Postural echo**
  Never underestimate the power of like-minded body signs.

Both these techniques are easy to do and much less risky to perform than all those hair-tossing, leg-rubbing flirt rituals.

Closing the Deal

It's no coincidence that the most popular first date is a meal for two in a cosy restaurant, or that there will be some form of dancing together prior to actual sex. Although several signals of attraction will be aimed at patterns of behaviour that have existed since your childhood (simply put, we can tend to be more attracted to people who resemble our opposite-sex parent in many subtle or more obvious ways) or mating potential and the production of healthy stock (nice teeth, hair, body shape, for example) or even the ability to protect (good bank-balance or muscles), we will also be correlating information about bedroom behaviour. In the early days of a relationship it can be considered brash to make verbal enquiries: 'Do you like to dominate?' 'Are you into gentle or rough sex?' 'Is your technique professional or are you inexperienced?' 'Will you be generous or self-centred?' but by watching a potential partner attack a plate of food or get boogying away on the dance floor there might be a barrel-load of information that we can tune into.

Eating

- If you're a messy eater you could imply you're messy or clumsy in bed.
- If you take a hands-on approach – like picking the food up or licking your fingers – you'll look like something of a sex maniac, someone who enjoys their sex but doesn't care much how they get it.
- If you burp or make noises you'll come across as the sort who farts in bed and thinks it's funny.

- If you eat quickly you'll register as an instant gratification type, someone who pounces but for whom it's all over in a flash.

- If you save the best bits to last, eating slowly and carefully, you'll come across as a delayed gratification type, someone who treats sex as a skill, with slow-build pleasure.

- If you eat food off your partner's plate you can either seem predatory and possessive or interested in your own needs in bed.

- If you make slurping noises you'll look like an uninhibited lover, but not necessarily in a good way.

- If you eat greedily your dinner partner might assume that sex is off the menu that night anyway. You're too busy filling up your stomach to compete in any sexual Olympics.

- If you're picky and leave lots of food you'll hint that you find sex distasteful and could be worried about messing up your hair.

- If you're analysing the menu to check for allergies and organic provenance you'll seem like the type of person to demand a full medical certificate before you even kiss goodnight.

Dancing

Dancing is probably the nearest thing to sex, which is why being a very bad dancer can be a huge turn-off. Although women will have an instinctive aversion for men who dance like a dad, they also have a deep distrust of men who twirl around the floor with too much conviction. The first will imply poor sexual technique and choreography and the second will suggest vanity and a little too much experience.

Merely displaying an ability to move to the beat of the

music is often sufficient to impress as it suggests passable choreography and an ability to tune into external rhythms, which is why many young women's hearts sank when they saw Prince William clapping woefully out of time at the concert for Princess Diana. Hopefully there was a delay on the timing between the music being played and the image hitting the screen, although that wouldn't explain how Harry and the rest of the royal box seemed able to keep to the beat we were hearing at home.

How to Kiss

We all know how to kiss, don't we? Yeah, right! This section is ostensibly for first-time kissers, but please feel free to show it to your partner of 20 years if appropriate, because it's never too late to learn.

There are several ways to do a good kiss. Some ways are nice and others are downright X-rated. Good kissing can be more difficult than actual penetrative sex. At least once you're having sex there's not too much in the way of subtlety to worry about, but the mouth and tongue are full of more sensitive nerve-endings, as well as the minefield that is the teeth, and because the mouth is part of the face and close to the ears and eyes your kissing technique will be more important as it can be very closely monitored.

The tip-toe kiss

This can be performed as part of the build-up to the real thing but it can also work by itself too. It's the least sexual-looking kiss but that doesn't mean it won't be a turn-on.

What it is: It's the gentlest of kisses because you only really brush lips together. It's fluttery rather than a full-on assault.

Why it's nice: It's very very flirty and can be extremely exciting, in a 'less is more' kind of a way.

How you do it: There should be some body contact to ensure perfect steerage as this kiss is especially hard to execute with no other touch. A hand to the chin or shoulders will do, then you pucker up very slightly but with no tightness or tension in the lips, which should be barely parted. Tilt your head gently to your right, close your eyes and do a series of very small kisses across your partner's lips. It's more of a nibble than a kissing movement, although needless to say no teeth are involved.

The guppy kiss

What it is: This kiss is popular with footballers taking the mickey or celebrities wanting to do a chaste-looking kiss for the cameras. It's a fun kiss that says as much about your shared sense of humour and confident sexuality as anything else.

Why it's nice: There's something essentially childlike about this kiss because it resembles the type of kiss very tiny kids will do when they're pushed together by adults and told to be nice.

How you do it: There should be no other bodily contact because that would spoil the joke. This kiss requires you to lean forward together with your lips fully puckered and meet square-on, without tilting your head or closing your eyes.

The regular kiss

What it is: It's good to know a regular-order kiss that will be acceptable to both parties. This is the middle-ground as far as kissing is concerned – nice, sexy but not too daring. A good first-date kiss.

Why it's nice: In kissing terms this is like the missionary position and you'll need to perfect it before you move on to anything more advanced. When someone's described as a good kisser it's usually this type of kiss they're known for, rather than anything more acrobatic.

How to do it: You'll need close proximity and lots of bodily touch, at least arms around one another or sitting side by side. The signal for this kiss will be close heads and matching eye contact – if your partner looks away then abort the mission because he or she's not interested. This kiss is all about someone taking the lead, though. If it's up to you, you should pause slightly with the eye-gaze. This is a difficult piece of body language to sustain, so your partner should be almost relieved when you stop gazing and start kissing.

Soften your eye expression as you move in for the kiss and tilt your head to your right a little. It's easier to kiss upward than it is to kiss downward so if you're a guy you could bend a little so your chin can be lifted. Not too far though, or she'll think you're shrinking. A slight jut of the lower lip as you come close aids direction and looks terribly sexy. Don't bare bottom teeth though or you'll look more like a werewolf.

The first kiss should be quite light and exploratory. Then you can increase the pressure while closing your eyes and pushing your torsos closer together. Your lips should part and turn clockwise slightly so your mouths join properly. At this point it would be okay to place one hand on the back of your partner's head but don't make it feel like a restraining gesture, just a light affectionate touch.

The best time to break is when the saliva becomes too unmanageable, which can be quite early on if you're inexperienced. Your mouths might make a noise as you kiss, which is okay, but you should never make a feature of it as it can be a turn-off if it gets too excessive. For this reason *never* suck as you kiss.

Clunking teeth is horrible but hard to avoid if you're new to kissing or a new couple. If it happens, back off a little bit until it's just lips again.

This type of kissing usually falls into the kiss-break-kiss-break pattern. If this happens, make sure you do your lighter kiss first each time before you go for the full-on snog.

French kissing

What it is: It's pretty much the same as the regular kiss, except your tongue joins in too.

Why it's nice: It's a more intense form of kissing and therefore more sexy because it mimics the actual act of sexual penetration. By using your tongue you get many more sensations, too.

How to do it: Go through all the steps in the regular kiss, but instead of breaking apart for small pauses, get even closer and more intense and gently poke your tongue into your partner's mouth. Like the exploratory smaller kiss this needs to be done subtly to start with if you want to be known for your good technique. A large tongue suddenly appearing in your open mouth can be an alarming experience but a tongue that waits for the go-ahead is usually more than acceptable.

Your tongue doesn't have a well-defined role once it is in the other mouth so don't busy it licking around teeth or doing flicky things like a snake. However, neither should it just lie there in the other person's mouth like a large slug taking a rest. Keep it moving in small, relaxed licking strokes. And remember the saliva rule – once you're welling up, it's time to break.

The romantic kiss

What it is: This kiss is mostly about the foreplay. Imagine you're going for the regular or the French kiss. Before you lock mouths you signal deep affection or love by adding some deft touches with your hands and eye contact.

Why it's nice: This is the type of kiss that can make a girl go weak at the knees – literally. It turns a kiss that could just mean lust into a meaningful kiss that could mean love. This is a delayed gratification kiss that suggests you're after your partner's mind and soul as well as their body. But be warned: if you do this kiss every time you meet a new partner you could easily be labelled a love rat.

How to do it: As you get close enough to kiss take a meaningful pause. Gaze deeply into his or her eyes and run a knuckle gently down the side of his or her face. This should be the index finger, bent into a crooked position, with the outside edge of the first joint used to do the touching. This gesture will signal you're amazed by them. Pause again and then cup your partner's face in both your hands, shrug your shoulders up together, tilt your head to your right, close your eyes and go straight for the deep, passionate kiss. There's no need for the reconnaissance mini-kisses with this kiss, as by holding his or her head in your hands you'll know you're on target without having to check.

The nose kiss

What it is: It's when the guy bends to plant a very delicate kiss on the tip of his girl's nose.

Why it's nice: It's good for two reasons: a) It's cute, and b) it doesn't mess up the lip gloss. It only really works if the girl's happy to be seen as a fluffy little bunnykins, but if that's cool, go for it.

How to do it: First you'll need to be considerably taller than your girlfriend and secondly you'll have to engage her full attention but without signalling that you want to kiss properly, otherwise she'll tilt her head up and the moment will be lost. The kiss needs to be light so you'll have to pucker. If you don't pucker you'll imply her nose is huge. David Beckham has famously used this nose kiss with his wife and it usually leaves other women going 'ahh' but without knowing exactly why.

The face-full of kisses

What it is: The guy plants small kisses all over the girl's face

Why it's nice: It's a rather old-fashioned and slightly chauvinistic kiss, but there's nothing wrong with the odd touch of machismo in the bedroom.

How you do it: Never perform this kiss if a woman's wearing carefully applied or heavy make-up. Take her face in your hands, regard her beauty for a moment or two then begin to plant small kisses across her face, starting with her forehead. Your lips should be lightly puckered but soft-ish.

How to Hold Hands

Hand-holding is important to a relationship as it tends to chart the stage a couple are at and their emotional and status compatibilities plus the state of their communications.

This is the classic form of hand-holding, implying a strong bond and a youthful approach to the relationship. The person with their hand on top in the clasp is usually the more dominant partner. The hands should be clasped firmly to imply sexual closeness. If the fingers are linked or entwined there's an even stronger desire to be seen as one unit.

This kind of hand-hold is a signature pose from the likes of the Beckhams. Although it places the male firmly in the dominant position, doing the leading, steering and protecting, it also creates something of a diva image for the female, making her look like the star while he takes on the role of bodyguard.

This is a much more traditional power-balance, with the guy in the dominant role while the woman becomes compliant to make the pose work.

This displays a huge status discrepancy. The guy's pose is independent and macho and the girl is having to make all the running to create the impression they're a couple. This suggests selfishness from the guy and submissiveness from the girl.

This is a difficult pose to carry off and walk at the same time, so the couple will register they're very much in tune and physically comfortable with one another. There's a large amount of status-equality in this pose, suggesting they both like to protect the other's back.

This pose will only work if the guy's much taller. It's an easy-going pose but with the guy stamping ownership on to his woman. If his shoulder hand is clutching her he's fiercely proud and protective but if his hand is just draped as though he's using her to prop up his arm, he's probably self-centred and a bit of a love rat.

This is the 'my hero' pose, possessive and proud, with the woman lowering her own status to the rank of a fan in an attempt to boost her guy's standing.

Ownership Signals

All couples have a way of beaming out their ownership signals. A possessive personality can often force these signals, causing discomfort to the other partner. Healthy ownership signals need to be evenly balanced and agreed, rather than enforced.

- **Grooming gestures**

  These strike genuine fear into the hearts of most men. It's that moment the woman picks a hair or piece of lint off his jacket or jeans, or rubs a mark off his face or smoothes his hair down for him. Even the smallest grooming gesture will promote the idea to the rest of the room that you're taken. It's hugely possessive and will cause panic in the groomee.

- **Tie-signs**

These subtle body language signals are almost invisible to the naked eye but they're the way that a couple communicates when they're not using words. Tie-signs are an important part of any close relationship but they're so instinctive and so subtle that often the couple aren't consciously aware they're using them.

A tie-sign can take several different forms: it can be a glance, a fast or slow blink, a mouth-gesture (like pulling the lips in to register disapproval), a narrowing or widening of the eyes, a head-tilt or nod, or a touch, tap or stroke. Tie-signs are examples of communication in a relationship and when one of the couple begins to ignore them you can bet good money the relationship is in trouble.

Negative tie-signs tend to be verbal. These are less agreed as signals and tend to have a lower hit rate. This always leads to arguments over misunderstandings, as in: 'When you asked if I was okay you should have known I wasn't by the tone of my voice' or 'I know I said I didn't want a birthday present but you should have been able to tell I didn't mean it.'

How to Tell if Your Partner is Lying

You know already – you know you do – it's probably just that it's often easier to collude with or believe the lie, or at least airbrush it away.

How do you know? Subconsciously and subliminally you'll have noticed subtle changes in your partner's body language and behaviour. The longer you've been together the more accurately you'll be able to spot these changes. This assumes, however, that your partner has been honest with you for most of your relationship. If they've been a compulsive liar from the start you could have more trouble spotting fluctuations, quite simply because there aren't any.

Tips to spot the liar

- First of all: ask yourself if you really do want to expose their lies. If you're happier being fooled then you might collude with the lie and only look for evidence of honesty.
- Value your gut reaction – it's based on very complex information processing.
- Remind yourself of your partner's normal, honest body language behaviours. Invest some time in studying them more closely to spot patterns of behaviour.
- Beware the error Othello made if you do decide to confront your partner. Being placed under pressure by being accused can produce shifty-looking body language signals in the most innocent person.
- Look for changes in normal behaviour, like working longer or different hours, more time spent away at courses or conferences, etc.
- Check for different smells. People having affairs often wash more or change their perfume or aftershave.
- They also buy new underwear.
- Their vocabulary changes as they pick up new words from their new love.
- As does their body language – look for new gestures.
- And don't overlook changes in their musical taste – they'll start to extend their CD collection.
- Don't be fooled if they start looking at you more. You might take this for affection but it's more likely they're evaluating you against their new lover.

- Don't expect nicer behaviour. Guilt will often make your partner more picky and argumentative. They're finding flaws in you so they don't feel as guilty.
- Look for extended pauses or playing for time if and when you ask questions.
- Watch for eye movement – it's not set in stone but eyes going up to the right can mean imagination or fabrication, to the left can mean recalled memory.
- Watch for cut-offs at the moment of lie, like dropping their eyes, looking away or face-covering.
- Watch for signs of increased pressure, which can cause an adrenalin buzz. This can mean a dry mouth with extra swallowing or lip-licking, shallow breathing, increased blink-rate and muscle tension of the jaw and shoulder area.

RED-CARPET KNOW-HOW – DOING RELATIONSHIP BODY LANGUAGE THE CELEBRITY WAY

I've been analysing celebrity body language for TV and magazines for several years and believe there's a lot we can all learn from their red-carpet poses. Celebrity double-acts are infamous money-spinners in a 'two-for-the-price-of one' way. This means there will always be a strong whiff of professionalism hanging around any celeb pairing, making it easy to be suspicious about the real messages behind the ones we see on display.

By reading a red-carpet couple's performed signals and then looking for their body language leakage you can gain some good insights into the state of some of your own relationships.

Bluff Displays

- As a general rule of thumb, the more affectionate a celebrity couple looks in public the nearer they are to a divorce. Remember Brad Pitt and Jennifer Aniston walking arm in arm along that tropical beach just before he rushed off into the arms of Angelina Jolie? Or Angelina's overt displays of tonsil tennis with hubby Billy Bob Thornton? When a couple try too hard to show their deep and enduring love for one another it's a sure bet their lawyers are busy licking the envelopes of the divorce papers.

- The hardest emotion to act out is a genuinely shared and very subtle sense of humour. I'm not talking about those full-on, mouth-thrown-wide-open smiles that you get from the likes of Katie Holmes and Britney Spears but the knowing smiles that a well-honed couple will throw one another to share a silent joke. These subtle and suppressed smiles will say more about what is positive in a relationship than any amount of full-on groping.

- Tie-signs are often invisible in photos but you can see them in action during filmed footage. When Tom Cruise appeared with Nicole Kidman when they were married he performed a series of small pats on her back as they were posing. These were behind-the-scenes pats as far as the banks of snappers were concerned but they showed how closely choreographed the couple apparently were and who was in charge of that choreography. Each pat Tom did appeared to be a signal for movement.

- Proximity is often a valuable clue to genuine red-carpet relationships. If a couple's heads are close there's often some trust on display. If their eye-gaze points in the same direction they're probably like-minded or share similar goals. Arm and hand displays are often easily performed but look for hidden hands that aren't held aloft but are clasped together. Torsos will be hugely revealing. If they're congruent, that is, both angled inward, the couple are probably for real, especially if there's pelvic closeness, which will signal a healthy sex life. Often though one person is turned full-on to camera while the other is draped over him or her. This is an ego and status display that can be telling. If it's the bigger star who's fronting the shots you can imagine some silent resentment from the partner. If it's the non-star who's fronting the pose while the big star plays compliant you'll know there's trouble to come.

- Some celeb couples manage a status imbalance but many more struggle. Look at footage or shots of Rod Stewart and Penny Lancaster and you'll see a big star employing submissive body language with his taller and more camera-friendly partner. At one stage Rod's response while Penny took over the interview was to ogle her cleavage to reinstate his alpha male credentials.

- Madonna and Guy inherited a huge status imbalance when they got together but so far they seem to have managed it impeccably. Guy is alpha in his own world of films but Madonna is undeniably the bigger name. When it's Guy's red-carpet occasion Madonna drops her own status signals dramatically, often hugging his back or torso like a devoted fan. When it's his wife's turn in the limelight Guy goes into 'bodyguard' mode, keeping a much more low-key look as he follows alongside.

- Some celebs appear to struggle with status-swings though. When Ben Affleck was dating Jennifer Lopez she was undeniably the bigger name. Instead of rocking and rolling with this at his movie premiere, though, Ben worked the crowd while J-Lo stood talking with what looked like security. It was obviously a bid to not upstage her man but a thousand cameras were still focused in her direction nevertheless. Ben had a very naughty habit when kissing Jennifer in front of the cameras, too, using what's called the distracted kiss. While kissing one of the world's most desirable women he would glance out and away from her, suggesting she wasn't enough to hold his attention.

- Elton John and David Furnish probably manage the red-carpet poses better than most. David excels at the perfect camera smile and they tend to pose as equals, with Elton marginally more dominant. As they move away from the cameras their tie-signs intensify rather than decrease, suggesting genuine affection.

- One big red-carpet moment that every celebrity dreads is the 'smile-you've-just-been-dumped' pose. Whereas normal mortals get to lock themselves away until the tears of shame have dried, recently dumped celebs are forced to grit their teeth and get out in front of the banks of cameras. Their response is always to perform what I call the Oscar-loser pose. Remember that moment during the Oscars when all the nominee faces are plastered on screen to see the response when they find out who won? The format is always the same: the winner must look distraught while the losers grin and laugh as though they've just heard some excellent news. When a close couple split there's no going back as far as their body language is concerned. All the naturally synchronised choreography ceases and they become less attuned than total strangers.

Key Points:

- There are many more cues for attraction than perfect good looks. Evolutionary impulses and positive body language signals can play a much larger role than beauty.
- Your facial expressions and body movements are far more likely to cause resonance than your outfit or hairdo.
- Your eyes will transmit and receive all those complex signals of attraction in the first few moments of meeting.
- A smile can be more seductive than any amount of self-touch or more overt sexual display.

10

HOW TO DEAL WITH FRIENDS AND RELATIVES

Dealing with partners and ex-partners can be a cinch compared with all those other relationships in our lives. Did you ever take time to consider your own body language signals when you're with parents, siblings, other relatives or friends? We tend to expect a form of unconditional love from most of these people in our lives, often basking in the knowledge that these are the people we can truly 'be ourselves' with, letting the social and/or workplace mask slip or drop with an almost audible sigh of relief.

Having relationships with people who know you well and who have seen you grow up so have a pretty accurate grasp of most facets of your personality makes us feel comfortable and secure. However it can also make us complacent, and complacency can lead to misunderstandings that cause rifts, rows and conflict.

Although you might save your prime performance moments in body language terms for lovers and people who have a direct effect on your career or bank-balance, it's just as vital to take steps to analyse and maximise your social or home 'performances' too. This chapter looks at the complex nature of those relationships and shows you some simple steps to help maintain or improve them.

POSITIVE BODYTALK

One of the best things about your body language with your friends is your instinctive tendency to perform postural echo. This is a natural mirroring of movement, mood and pace that can even have the effect of making friends look like one another. Sometimes it's contrived to send a conscious signal of pack formation and exclusivity to the rest of the world. An example of this is when school kids create their own gestures and language and clothing style that – although not exclusive to their pack and probably copied from others in the first place – will still be worn as a kind of badge to denote similarities within their group.

When two close friends greet one another there are usually mirrored rituals, with changes in facial expression and displays of hugging, patting and even punching or hitting that would never be used between strangers. It's polite to greet friends in this intimate way but it can be less usual to greet family members with such gusto.

Sadly, the very fact that you feel less pressure to 'put your best face forward' with close family members can lead to upset or conflict. As much as we cherish the ability to 'be ourselves' with family, that non-performed 'self' can be wearing to live with. Any parent who has ever watched their teenage offspring's communications range from open, positive and friendly with their peers to monosyllabic and negative with them will know the feelings of anger, frustration, bewilderment and rejection that occur as a result. What should really be flattering – the fact that the teen has no feelings of pressure to mask their depression and bewilderment at life in general when with their parents – becomes perceived as an insult. The same is true of many close family relationships. Without the perceived need for social masking a very unpleasant-looking 'real' self can emerge.

It's perhaps important to remember that we were all once egocentric children who only saw our own needs and wants and had no thoughts of social performing. This child is still very much alive and well inside ourselves and we can happily revert to that same state when we're feeling safest and most relaxed.

A colleague's elderly father was recently disabled. Whenever she visited she would sit listening to a catalogue of moans and descriptions of the levels of depression he was suffering. Yet when she bumped into the next-door neighbour she was told how bright and upbeat her father was and how well he was braving his disablement, always laughing it off. My colleague quite naturally felt resentment. Why did she get all the moans while everyone else got this upbeat performance? The answer is an easy one, but dealing with this incongruence is probably less easy. Do relatives always get the worst of their family members? The answer is probably yes. Family relationships can be very selfish because that's the framework they're based on. At one time a parent or older sibling would have had the job of nurturing the younger child and offering it unconditional love. This state is very seductive and it's one we seek to replicate throughout our entire lives. This means being loved in spite of our behaviour, not the demanding, exhausting social mask we use on everyone else.

Hierachy and Pecking Orders

Every family is hierarchical and it can be this strong pecking order that is necessary for peace. Age and wisdom are the most valid reasons for high status within the unit but, like any colony of animals, the question of age dominance is no longer a given once the children get to physical maturity.

There's always an underlying sense of alpha supremacy in a family group, where the status is usually decided by size and strength. Often parents take a short-term view when they establish this. Kids grow very quickly and each generation seems to get bigger and taller, which can lead to the kind of face-offs that you normally only see in a wildlife setting.

Avoiding status squabbles

- Throughout the early life of your child try to avoid body language gestures that emphasise height, size or power differentials like looming over someone, placing your hands on your hips, shouting or blocking their way. These can come back and bite you.
- Use real signals of intellectual power instead. Keep calm and use assertive body language like eye contact (though not hard staring), open, emphatic but unswerving gestures and physical confidence rather than underlying aggression.
- Many if not most family squabbles are prompted by status incongruence. In an animal colony this would be sorted out by fighting but, luckily, humans are usually less willing to gouge, claw and wrestle to establish the pecking order. Always remember that no hierarchy is ever totally stable. People leave home and get promoted in the workplace, family members age and the nurturers and protectors become the ones needing to be cared for. Status squabbles in families focus around seating and sleeping arrangements, space, food, fairness and tokens of power like the remote control or car keys.

- Parents often try to succumb to these constant battles by dividing rather than ruling. If each family member has his or her own space with their own TV and computer the status battles appear to vanish at one stroke. With its own remote control and mouse in its hand a child can feel in charge of its own destiny. Unfortunately destiny isn't all about life on screen. By sidelining children (and adults!) in this way, they can miss out on real life and the vital lessons that need to be learnt for survival. Because of the computer an entire generation has grown up wielding false feelings of grandeur and power. Having had their own space and virtual kingdom for most of their growing years, but without ever learning the skills of real status or transactional development, this generation could end up in trouble. Even bad transactions are better than no transactions at all as no communication means no learning.

- In body language transactions among family members or even close friends there is often a parent/adult/child ratio that can cause transactional success or transactional failure. How many of us have had arguments with our parents for 'still talking to me as though I'm a child'? And how many parents have felt aggrieved when their adult child fails to treat them with respect any more?

- It's very rare for family members to use the adult-to-adult behaviour and body language that we learn to strive for in our business relationships. This is where both people are acting in a way to imply even status and using calm and unprejudiced language. In fact this style of communication would be almost unnatural in a family setting, where there will always be a perception of pecking order.

Emphasised child displays may include:

- Shouting
- Stamping
- Clenched fists
- Folded arms to signal rebellion or stubbornness
- Waving someone away
- Shrugging
- Cut-offs, like face-covering or shutting eyes
- Crying
- Sticking out of bottom lip or jaw-jutting
- Curling into self, hunching, head down
- Door-slamming
- Giggling
- Wrestling
- Play-fighting

Emphasised parent displays may include:

- Finger-pointing or wagging
- Staring
- Hands on hips
- Body-blocking
- Standing with legs astride
- Head-shaking or head-baton
- Tutting
- Rolling eyes
- Puffing
- Nurturing, e.g. stroking, hugging, ruffling hair, wiping face, grooming gestures, offering food, etc.

CREATING COMPLEMENTARY BEHAVIOURS

Much will depend on whether these body displays are complementary or not. Often the problems come when a parent displays parental gestures in front of his or her child's friends or peers, thus lowering a child's status in a pack it needs to survive in. Remember the kids getting a kiss from their mums at the school gate? That kiss was probably sought at home but will spell doom for the child when it's performed in front of its peers. Complementary body language transactions are ones that assume compatible roles. For instance, when a parent tells a child to 'Tidy your room' and uses staring and finger-wagging to make its point, the parent is adopting a critical, dominant role which will seek out a submissive, compliant response. If the child says, 'Okay, sorry, Dad,' hanging their head, dropping their eyes and rushing upstairs with a dustpan and brush, the transaction will have been complementary. If the child rushes into the lounge yelling: 'It's nearly Christmas!' waving their arms and smiling, that child is firmly in instinctive, enthusiastic child mode. To make this a complementary transaction the parent would need to respond in kind, e.g.: 'Yay! I can't wait either!' and start running round the room and laughing.

But what happens when the first scenario obtains a non-complementary response? What if the first kid stares back at its parent, juts its chin and says nothing? This will be the child going into stubborn rebellious mode and it means the parent will need to go to stage two. Or what if the second kid gets a response of 'Don't interrupt me while I'm reading' and is mock-swatted away with one flick of the hand? Chances are that the child will look disappointed and a chance for building closeness between parent and child will have been missed.

Pushing the Transaction

Creating complementary body language transactions isn't always useful though. If your best mate has a habit of raising her status and ordering you around and telling you what to do, you can take a complementary stance by adopting a subservient pose, dropping your posture and doing what you're told, but – unless you have a predilection for servitude – you'll probably feel a building resentment each time you act compliant.

It's very possible, then, that you will want to make moves to change your friend's behaviour. Instead of the compliant, complementary response you might opt for something less servile that will make her less likely to dominate you. It would be tempting to try an aggressive stance, staring hard and pointing as you accuse her of bossing you around. This is likely to force her even further into the controlling state by getting angry and arguing. Strategic body language plotting means you'd opt for an assertive state, keeping calm and adult as you use enough eye contact to look confident and enough open, emphatic gestures to show you don't want to argue but you mean what you say.

These strategic body language transactions can help with any social or family relationship. Transactional planning is especially useful if you're locked into a transactional pattern with one or more relatives – i.e. a kind of 'Groundhog Day' scenario when you always argue over the same things. You could have a disagreeable mother-in-law who you feel is always criticising you when she comes to visit or a sibling who's always getting drunk and acting like a child at weddings or parties. Once you pinpoint their body language state by studying their gestures, posture and facial expressions you can analyse if you're going for the complementary response (which could include arguing, paying too much attention to them or getting upset and crying) or if you should try to change your state to persuade them to change theirs.

PRACTICAL TIPS TO AVOID FLASHPOINTS WITH FAMILY OR FRIENDS

The next few pages contain some very practical tips for creating empathy and rapport with the people closest to you. They might involve changing some of your traditional patterns of behaviour and they can be read as a 'pick and mix', i.e. you pick out what you feel fits your own scenarios, but do read them with an open mind, especially if you have traditional flashpoints or trouble spots that you want to overcome.

How to Meet Your New Partner's Family and Friends for the First Time

Meeting a new partner's loved ones can be daunting, but not always for the reasons everyone imagines. It would be a cliché to suggest you want to make a good first impression, but there should always be limits. Being too ingratiating at first can cause problems later on in this relationship, and although it's fine to lower your own status to a certain degree in order to integrate with your new partner's loved ones, anything more radical may mean you're forced into a low-status role for the rest of your life together.

First there are a few things you need to keep in mind about his or her family and friends' thoughts towards you. They have history with this person you've fallen for. Many of the family and friends group will see you as a rival. One of their key concerns will be that you might dominate and change your new partner. They also know that they're being saddled with you through no choice of their own. You're looking at what is probably a very tight-knit group that has formed over a very long space of time and you're about to penetrate it. If you don't they might lose one of their group members.

This is why some form of grovel-display is vital, but at the same time you don't want to look as though you're 'not good enough' for your partner.

Tips for integrating with family or friends

- Ask to see photos of all the key players before you meet them.
- Find out who the alphas are in the group. Who is the lead relative or who is the pack leader among the friends? They're the only ones you really need to impress.
- Never take a gift on first meeting. It will look as though you're trying to buy your way in. Or get your partner to give the gift instead.
- Dress marginally more formally than the group you're meeting. It shows respect.
- Use limited ingratiation or submission signals. When you first walk in keep an upright posture but apply a really winning smile (see the smile advice in Chapter Seven).
- Perform a very small 'bow' when you greet each person. This is symbolic bowing rather than the formal type, and will involve dropping your torso slightly or dipping your head very subtly (see Chapter Eight).
- Allow yourself to display a maximum of two signs of nerves or shyness. This will signal respect.
- Use good eye contact. It will be your best intentional gesture, looking as though you're keen to get to know each person.

- Play Follow My Leader. Never push the group behaviour during the first few meetings. If they look miserable keep it like that, don't try to get them laughing by telling your worst jokes. If they seem prudish or formal don't swear or make risqué comments. If they're light-hearted don't start fishing for more in-depth conversations. You're the interloper and as such you should never seek to change the dynamics. Use mirroring and postural echo with the people you're trying to impress.

- Don't show off in an attempt to impress.

- Keep affection and sex signals completely toned down. Just opt for the Look of Love – that is, face-softening.

- Never flirt with an in-law. It might flatter the parent but your partner will be appalled, even if it's done in fun.

- Never diss your partner. Not even if the others are hacking them about by teasing and ribbing. This is a rite of passage – they're flexing their ownership muscles to see how you respond. If you join in you'll display disloyalty. However, if you stand up for your mate you could alienate the rest of the group. Play it right down the middle. Smile politely, face-check your partner to see how he or she is doing and say nothing.

- Ditto when the baby snaps come out. This is a rite of passage with most people's parents. Smile and say how cute he or she looks. Throw a wink at your partner when no one else is looking.

- Never whisper to your partner or do eye tie-signs in front of friends and family. This signals a private conversation and will imply you're trying to take him or her away from them.

As you leave from your first meeting you need to hope that your exit salutations are less formal than those you did on arrival. This is where you'll be hoping for a hug or extra arm-squeeze that lets you know you've been accepted. Even if you get them, though, take nothing for granted. Friends and family could just be performing these in a bid to impress their offspring or mate. They might know you're possibly in for the long haul and that if they declare war at this stage they'll look mean-spirited. If your in-laws seem especially poisonous you should also remember that the more fulsome their hugs and signals of affection the more they're going to slag you off once you're gone.

Although it should be natural for a person to want to mate with someone who will integrate into their own family unit, you could find out that you're dating a 'Mummy-shocker' rather than a 'Mummy-pleaser'. This will mean that your character and appearance have appealed to your partner for the very reason that their parents won't approve. Sometimes you'll have no warning of this and be blissfully unaware until you meet the parents, at which point you'll be amazed to discover they're not also Goths or hippies and have no great liking for recreational drugs. If this happens there is probably very little point in trying to integrate with them as that's not what you're there for. You've been selected as a tool of revenge for all those humiliations your partner had growing up and it's up to you if you want to be used in this way or if you'd rather take yourself off to a relationship that is less Oedipal.

How to do weddings and parties

Hell should freeze over before you allow yourself to get drunk at any social event organised by your partner's friends or family. Being 'the outsider' is a role that can stick for years, at the very least until another member of the group pitches up with a new mate who is undeniably worse than you. No matter how well integrated you feel you should always keep the thought in mind that you are penetrating your partner's group and therefore contain any 'leading' behaviour until you're back with your own pack.

Stay marginally more low-key and low-status with your body language at social events and display good manners with your partner at all times.

The secrets to good wedding/party body language are:

- Look genuinely happy when you arrive as the entire room will be casting their beady eyes in your direction. Walking in with a face like a slapped arse for whatever reason is just not good enough. Keep in mind that any big family gathering will always include several elderly relatives, or people suffering in silence, or those on the edge – waiting for their waters to break, for example. Your weaned-on-a-pickle face won't gain you any Brownie points when you follow that lot into church.

- Listen, don't speak. The core skill of any social function is to produce active listening signals and use them on everyone. Eye contact, nodding, head-tilts, mirroring...all you need to do is to prompt people with open questions and then go into full-attention mode.

- Never become overcongruent. Exaggerated niceness will offend as it looks phoney and patronising. Just because someone is either elderly and/or drunk doesn't mean you shouldn't talk to them as though they're an adult.

- Act like a royal. When members of the royal family go on visits they have an assistant running beside them to whisper appropriate bits of information to them about each person they will be meeting. Your partner should be pressed into service for this duty, enabling you to begin conversations with lines like: 'Ah, Caroline, aren't you the aunt who got into the finals of *The Weakest Link* four years ago?' or 'Colin? Not the Colin with the allotment near the flyover?' etc.

Greeting Your Own Family

Even though it's good to mirror close friends and relatives there's often a chicken-and-egg scenario when it comes to meeting and greeting your own loved ones. Although it's always nice to be yourself it's also probably better to get rid of that glum-looking screensaver face before you greet your loved ones. It's easy to pitch up at your parents' house and walk in moaning about the journey down. It's also easy to forget they probably spent several hours – if not days – preparing for your visit. They then mirror your glum mood and it's downhill all the way from there.

One friend told me her mother would always greet her in adulthood with the words 'You don't look very happy!' My friend would then reply, 'Neither do you!' and it was frosty faces from then on. Who was in the wrong? Like most family squabbles, the answer is probably no one. All it needed was for one person (my friend in this case) to bite the bullet and change a very small communication trait to break the negative pattern of behaviour. Next time she met her mother she smiled and looked pleased to see her. Her mother responded and peace was restored.

How to Delegate Housework

Housework can come high up on the list of aggro-inducers in any household, with only money topping it as the reason why fights break out. In a perfect world all household tasks should be lovingly and keenly performed with every family member taking his or her share. Unfortunately this is so rarely the case I have to admit I have never seen the system in action. What usually occurs is that one person seems to take ownership of all the household tasks and then tries to delegate them, leading to accusations of nagging and a constant need to keep re-delegating every time the chore crops up.

Task delegation in the household can be tricky, especially if you're going to avoid the three key forms of failure:

1 Verbal repetition: often seen as nagging.
2 Giving up and doing it yourself: turns the 'delegater' into a compliant doormat.
3 Getting other family members to do the tasks but with the attitude that they are your jobs that you will always have to ask them to do: victim still retains ownership of ghastly task and anyone doing them considers themselves to be doing him or her a favour.

Ideally your family should understand the tasks are for the benefit of all and decide themselves to do them when they need doing, not wait to be asked or expect to be thanked. Here are some tips to help achieve this ideal situation:

- Always communicate face-to-face when you can have undivided attention. Ideally all family members need to be present.
- Employ body language that oozes confidence and authority. Avoid any Power Posturing but a calm posture, good eye contact and a confident delivery are vital.

- Don't begin the conversation by airing past gripes. 'You've never lifted one finger to help in seven years' is a very weak gambit because this is something they can't change. Do you want an apology or do you want action? Too many goals, especially emotional goals tangled up with behaviour goals, will cause confusion.
- Never allow emotion to show in your vocal tone or your body language. If they can hear you're upset they'll smell first blood.
- Sit slightly higher than the rest of the family – perching on the edge of the table is better than sitting on a low settee.
- If they fight back, don't back down. Fiddling, looking away, face-touching or arm-folding will all look like defensive signals.
- Listen to their points and don't interrupt. Then pause. Then stick to your guns.
- Don't make threats. Kids can always threaten better and carry their threats out.
- When your children or partner do the tasks never stand over them shouting out rules and instructions or ridiculing. Encouragement and praise are more motivational but never thank them – it gives ownership of the task to you for ever.

When you relate to friends and family it's probably true to say that you are as near to 'being yourself' as you can get. These transactions will work on a completely different level to those you have with colleagues or even sexual partners as you're dealing with people who you have known or who have known you probably from birth. However this doesn't guarantee that all your transactions will be successful, in fact far from it. Your friends/family behaviours have been learned from a very early age but that doesn't mean there's no scope for change. As with nearly everything else in the book, I've looked at small changes that can make the maximum difference. Just a tiny diversion from your normal, programmed response could make a massive difference to the results you achieve.

FRIENDS REUNITED

Some last thoughts and tips specifically on friendships. However close your friends are, there is one huge difference between them and your family and that is the issue of unconditional love or bonding. Although families can and do split up, blood relatives tend to stay with you for ever. Not so friends, which is why you should never take them for granted. Remember that great set of close pals you had at your last job? What happened when you or they moved on? No matter how many work colleagues swear to stay in touch it's commonly found that they will lose touch once the common bond (the job) no longer exists. Childhood friendships are often scuppered by marriage and a huge modern problem is one of property or career moves taking people off to live abroad.

It helps to analyse your friendships to discover what works, why it works and how to cherish it rather than taking it for granted.

- A key ingredient of bonding with friends is image and body language. For comfort and animal security reasons we tend to like people who look or act like us. School tends to create some superficial bonds like this. At school you were placed with children of your own age who nearly all lived locally. Often the financial backgrounds of school kids will be relatively similar, and the school experience means you are working on the same tasks. Children are great body language mimics and will often copy one another extensively, creating strong rapport. Some school groups will dress alike, talk alike and move alike in a bid to make their bonds even stronger. This pack identity is a big factor in who we mix with and who we don't.

- Without regular face-to-face contact to maintain these visual ties a friendship can weaken, especially if the similarities were superficial to start with. Although text and email are good ways of keeping in touch, always remember you'll need constant 'mimic' sessions, i.e. face-to-face meets, to maintain strong bonds.

- If there has been a gap in this contact, use telephone conversations to reboot vocal and verbal pattern ties rather than sending photographs or video links. If your tie-signs have diminished on these links so will your rapport. When you speak on the phone you at least have a chance to use verbal mirroring to create empathy and rapport.

- Never assume that your friends will all like one another. At school you had groups or gangs but your friends as an adult will probably come from a mixture of sources. They will look and seem similar to you but never forget how much you and they will have flexed to create those friendships. What you might think is just pure luck – i.e. that you know so many people with things in common – is actually the result of a strong and complex social bonding process that will have involved massive behavioural flexing that you were possibly consciously unaware of. So friends that you love might easily hate one another, or find they have very little in common apart from you. One sign of this is the way guests at weddings often run out of conversation once they've asked one another: 'How do you know the bride/groom?'

- It also helps to be consciously aware of the 'pecking order' of your friendships. Like every other relationship in your life there will be compatible behaviours that are maintained to keep the peace. If you have a 'gang' or pack you socialise with frequently it will be useful to study the individual roles in that group, and see if they are flexible. Is there an alpha? Do some of you adopt submissive/compliant roles or stances, and if so is that comfortable or irritating?

- Hierarchical groups mean peaceful groups in the animal kingdom, although there can still be challenges for power or control. The point about animals though is that they seem to be very aware of who's in charge and what their own role is in the hierarchy. Humans are often less aware and this can destabilise friendship groups.

- Partnerships with the opposite sex can also threaten or destabilise friendships, which is why pals often try to split relationships up by joking about or ridiculing them once they start to sound serious. This is partly caused by a sense of loss that can build almost to the point of mourning by the time a couple tie the knot. Crying at weddings isn't always about happiness.

- Be aware of the body language rituals involved when a friend pairs off with a mate. By turning a subconscious process of approval or rejection into a conscious process you could prevent a friendship breaking up for ever. Your friend's new partner is unlikely to arrive on the scene with body language that is compatible to your own. He/she might even have made radical changes to your friend's body language patterns, meaning he/she feels like a virtual stranger. The common ritual is to try to see or create a body language match with the newcomer so that they have a chance of integration. Otherwise they could be rejected. This initiation can even involve unconscious flirting with him/her in an attempt to change their body language approach. Many friendships split up because one friend appears to be flirting with another's partner. Although this needn't be innocent it is, ironically, often prompted by a strong desire for pack acceptance.

- Be constantly aware of your friendship mirroring as it really is the ties that bind. Change is a constant factor in all our lives and change can often strengthen friendships, but only if the core similarities are in place. Discover these core values in all your friendships and work to maintain them.

Key Points:

- Although you might cherish the need to be yourself at home and with your family, always remember that 'self' is still multi-faceted and you should never place your own needs above everyone else's.
- It's important and still possible to create complementary transactions with your family. Even though behaviour patterns have been in place for many years, you can still change your own behaviours to get a more effective response or result.
- Use body language tricks like active listening signals and postural echo to create a good impression at social events.

PART FOUR: BODY LANGUAGE AND BUSINESS

This section of the book is all about workplace skills that are relevant to any career. Jobs tend to divide into two key sets of competencies: your ability to do tasks and your ability to communicate, motivate, impress, sell, influence and even entertain. Body language is a vital component of this last list of qualities.

11

GETTING ON BOARD – THE SKILLS OF RECRUITMENT AND INTERVIEWS

A job interview is one of the most important body language performance moments in your life. Unless you're a professional poker player I seriously doubt there will ever be so much money hanging on so brief an encounter.

The very worst advice you will ever be given about interviews is this:

'Just be yourself.'

Anyone who says this to you is wrong, wrong, wrong. Job interviews are formal and false and chock-full of rituals. You'll have to get gussied up and sit alone in a chair in a smallish room being questioned by a group of people you've never seen before in your life. Therefore there is no 'yourself' in this particular scenario.

What you will need to do is to look like the person they are looking for. How many companies do you think are actively scouring the land for you as you really are? This isn't Prince Charming clutching a glass slipper, it's a company wanting to recruit someone who will make a difference to their profits or output. 'Just be yourself' means no planning, no rehearsing and no real effort. Now as much as I hate clichés, I'm duty-bound to throw a couple in your direction right now, which you should keep in mind when getting ready for a job interview: 'No pain, no gain' and 'To fail to prepare is to prepare to fail.'

I'm not asking you to change everything about yourself, but a bit of polishing, buffing and tweaking never harmed anyone's chances.

Ten Things You Need to Know About Applying for a Job

1 The recruiters *could* have hired you from your CV and qualifications alone. The fact they didn't means they intend to judge you by appearance and performance at interview. Your first impression could be vital.

2 They're looking to see if you appear 'normal'. So keep those polka-dot socks for another day.

3 They're looking to judge your personality. If you get the job you'll need to fit in with the existing team.

4 They're looking to see how you might handle work-place scenarios. Expect a little role-play or hypothetical questions.

5 They could be just as nervous as you are.

6 They're on the same side as you – they want you to be fabulous. Recruitment interviews are costly, time-expensive and reasonably dull. They're desperate for you to press all their buttons and tick all their boxes. Assume they will begin by liking you and that this 'liking' will continue until you prove them wrong.

7 You could be 'on view' before you even reach the premises. Without wishing to get too Big Brother on you, remember things like security cameras.

8 Your key moments will be your entrance and your exit. Both will create the most lasting impressions.

9   The more interviews you do, the better you should get. Only your emotional response will scupper your chances. If you start to get demotivated (albeit quite naturally) and discover a talent for self-loathing, the chances are this will show in your body language signals. Instead, use each interview as experience. Like driving a car, the more you do it the better you will get.

10 An interview is your chance to shine but it's not your chance to hog the limelight. You have two ears, a brain and one mouth. Use them in roughly that proportion. Listen – think – talk. Listen – think – talk. Listen – think – talk. Your interviewers will be keen to discover your capacity for learning, understanding and taking instructions. There are very few interviews where the objective is to book someone with verbal diarrhoea. And listen to the question. I've been in the situation where you ask one question and – because the interviewee has failed to listen – they answer something else. You'd be amazed how often this happens.

Planning Stages

I know this is a book about body language, but if you don't plan your answers to some of the killer questions you might get asked, your body language signals are extremely likely to suffer as a result.

You will never be able to guess all their questions with any huge degree of accuracy, but it's a bit of a no-brainer to assume there will be some about your past experience, your values, your interests and your desire for and commitment to the job on offer.

If you're inexperienced you'll need to talk about any relevant experiences like part-time work, work experience or even hobbies and interests.

If you are experienced expect to trawl though jobs you've done in the past and reasons for leaving your present or last job.

Modesty is a pretty useless value to bring to the interview but so is arrogance. You need to get the balance right, and to do that you need to be able to show the interviewers that you are the best person for the job.

Proving Yourself

An increasing number of companies in the UK will give applicants a trial run for a couple of weeks to see how they do. This technique tends to be limited to fast-learn jobs like café or shop work where talent, or lack of it, will emerge quite quickly. Unfortunately the same will hardly apply to jobs like accountancy or marketing where there is a much slower build-up of basic skills. So how can you prove to the interviewer that you have what it takes? The answer is that you will stand a much better chance of getting the job if you're the living, breathing epitome of all the skills required. Which takes us back to one of the core messages of this book:

SHOW, DON'T TELL

You can list all your dazzling skills like honesty, team-leadership, communications and management but if you don't display you don't get the pay. There are two ways to display your talents:

1 Back up all your claims with hard proof.
2 Look and act the part.

You will, of course, need to do both.

- When you tell your interviewer you have leadership/
  management skills, follow your claim up by telling them
  when and how you have used them.
- When you tell them you're keen to be employed by their
  company, prove your point by displaying knowledge of
  them and their products or services.
- When you say you have people skills, show them by using
  them on the interviewers.

It's amazing how many applicants miss this one very simple
trick. They will happily turn up late for the interview then claim
they're 100 per cent reliable. They'll answer questions in mono-
syllables but then claim they could charm the birds from the
trees in terms of selling. They boast about their presentation
skills but struggle over simple introductions. Take proof of all
your claims. Be ready to cite examples and give evidence.

Plan your physical choreography. First impressions – your
blink factor – will count during an interview like never before.

Set Your Goals

It's no good just performing 'better body language'. Without
setting out some image targets you'll be floundering rather than
directive. If you've read an ad for the job, re-read it to discover
clues about the type of person they're looking for. Are there any
descriptive terms like 'ambitious', 'friendly', 'organised', 'capable',
'outgoing'? If so you already have a good part of your image map
made out for you. If you've been sent by an agency then do remember to ask what was said when the job came on to their books.
Why have you been sent? What qualities did the client ask for?

Once you're prepared to align yourself with the specifica-
tions you should then decide what else you'll be bringing to

the party. What personal qualities do you feel you should be advertising? Set yourself a list then create a profile from that list. For instance you might have:

From the job spec
- Hard-working
- Friendly
- Outgoing

From your own list
- Intelligent
- Fast-learning
- Diligent

Keep personal qualities like 'sense of humour' in reserve; see how the interview pans out before you try something like this on the interviewers.

All these qualities should be displayed visually as well as verbally. Once you have created your image map, try to think a little like an actor getting into a role. Compare reality with your 'ideal'. For instance, are you really shy or anxious about the interview but want to look outgoing and confident? Or are you really outgoing but with a tendency to go quiet on first meetings?

This is the moment for some reflection on what's called image discrepancy, the difference between how you really are or how you think you could be, and how you *currently* come across to other people. Interviewers are busy people. If a quality doesn't jump out and bite them, they'll usually assume you don't have it.

Likeability

What makes someone likeable at interview stage? Likeability is random but there are some patterns that you can use for your benefit.

1   We tend to like people who are like us. Therefore your mirroring techniques will be vital. Be alert throughout the interview, too. The interviewers' body language or communication might change. They could relax or become more friendly and chatty. These are called cues. You should take them as an invitation to follow suit, although 'follow' is the operative word. Never take the lead, as it's not your role to change the mood of the meeting by taking control.

2   Gestures that are directed out towards your audience will make them like you more. These are inclusive gestures, rather than exclusive. People have the same liking for animated facial expressions, especially if they include similar inclusive tie-signs that speak directly to an audience.

3   People like people who talk their own language. If you can pick up on any of their terms or jargon they'll tend to find it easier to like you.

Here's the list of inclusive as opposed to exclusive gestures.

Inclusive gestures
- Catching someone's eye then smiling
- Smiling when they speak or make a joke
- Leaning forward
- Nodding
- Using hands held out in the empty embrace – that is, held

out slightly towards the audience, raised to waist height, held apart with palms facing
- Open gestures with palms showing
- Legs crossed towards your audience

Exclusive gestures
- Looking down
- Closing your eyes in a long blink
- Smiling to yourself
- Poker face – no expression
- Folded arms and crossed legs
- Legs crossed away from your audience
- Appearing self-absorbed via fiddling, self-grooming or studying your nails
- Looking down while shaking your head
- Chewing
- Tapping
- Leaning back in your chair

Rehearse the inclusive gestures before the interview so that they appear natural. And be aware of the exclusive gestures you do and try to break yourself out of the habit. Here are some more body language pointers that will help you land that dream job.

Physical preparation
- Get an early night. If you're too nervous to sleep, make yourself lie still with your eyes shut.
- Take exercise for the couple of days before the interview. Nothing too strenuous, just enough to make you look energetic and vigorous.
- On the morning of your interview get up at least half an

hour earlier than you think you should. Drink orange juice, only eat light foods and don't smoke. The smell of greasy or cooked foods and cigarettes shouldn't be hanging on you when you walk in.

- Use only very light cologne or perfume. No one likes an employee who smells like a skunk. Everyone has different tastes and your loving of Eau de Musk might not be shared universally.

- Do use an anti-perspirant deodorant.

- Your hair should look freshly washed and tidy. If it's long, tie it back or it could fall over your face if you get shy.

- Always be freshly shaved. No stubble. Beards are hugely controversial too. Sport one at your peril unless you're applying for a job at a ZZTop convention.

- Turn up at least 10 minutes before the interview time, longer if it's with a big company with a complex security system.

- If possible, hang around near the company before your interview to find out what employees are wearing and dress slightly more formally than they do.

- Go online to find out everything you can about the company and its products. Never assume you know a company just because you see its name often – big brand names often have subsidiaries that make totally different products.

- During your wait at reception always act as though you're in the actual interview. Sit well and be polite. If possible thumb through company magazines that are often left on reception tables.

- If there are other applicants waiting, don't sit demotivating yourself by trying to work out who looks better than you do. Take a copy of *The Times*, folded to the cross-word. Pretend to fill it in and pretend to time yourself when you pretend to finish. It always out-psychs the opposition.

- If possible, go to the loo when you arrive to check your hair, straighten your tie, check your flies, etc.

- Take a businesslike bag only, no handbags or carrier or plastic bags.

- Carry your bag in your left hand so the right is free for handshakes.

- Practise your sitting and standing body language at home in front of the mirror, wearing your interview outfit.

- Keep pockets stitched up to prevent you from stuffing your hands into them.

- Never have a balled tissue shoved up your sleeve.

- Take a moment before you walk into the interview room. Run through your Power Pose.

- Enter the room well. Step into the room, in front of the door, and close it behind you without looking back.

- Smile and shake but let them offer their hand first. If they don't offer, don't bother.

- Always offer a firm, cool, dry hand. If you get sweaty, wipe it with a baby wipe before you go into the room.

- Try to shake hands with everyone in the room.

- Use eye contact as you shake.

- Wait to be offered a chair before you sit down. If they forget, ask first.

- You can move your chair slightly. Turn it towards the interviewers or move it slightly further forward if it seems too far away. Never pull it right up to their desk as though you're about to eat lunch.

- Never touch their desk or place anything on it. If you're at a board table you can place your hands or notes on the table.
- Sit into the back of the chair, back upright but not rigid and legs lightly crossed. Place your elbows on the armrest and lightly clasp your hands on your lap.
- Use active listening skills when they talk.
- Use a listening and thinking pause before you answer each question. This will make your answers appear honest rather than slick. Flick your eyes downward and slightly to your left. This will look reflective. If you raise your gaze to the ceiling or even upward you could appear to be stumped by the question, or to be making your answer up.

Active listening

- Use 100 per cent eye contact.
- Nod as they talk. Pace your nodding to match their style of delivery.
- Never interrupt.
- Keep focused on their key points.
- Mirror their body language and facial expression.
- Don't fiddle or tap.
- Lean forward slightly if they talk for a long time.
- Never use a 'parking' gesture, like raising a finger slightly and holding it there to signal you have a point you want to make.

Gestures That Will Impress or Depress at an Interview

Impressive

Legs crossed, elbows on arms of chair.

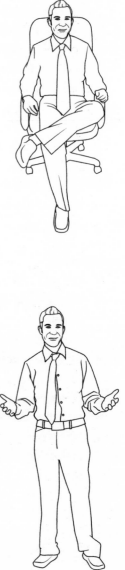

Legs slightly open (only if
you're wearing trousers,
of course!).

Open gestures, both hands out but not overcongruent.

Precision gestures – fingers of one hand pinched together, pointing upward.

Palms-up gestures.

Fingers lightly linked.

Leaning forward slightly when you're asked a question, which makes it look as though you're keen to reply, even if you don't know the answer.

Depressive

Legs and arms crossed.

Rubbing back of neck
with one hand.

Face-touching.

Legs crossed and turned away
from interviewer so that leg closest
to interviewer forms a barrier.

Bag still on lap.

Fig-leaf pose.

Perched on edge of
chair with feet tucked
away right under the chair.

Sitting back in chair, slightly slumped, legs splayed,
one finger on face.

Saying Goodbye – The Subtle Art of Exit Impressions

You may feel as though your interview has gone well, or you might fear it's gone rather badly. Generally it's almost impossible to gauge your chances of success unless you know you've been especially awful and called the interviewer's wife a baboon-bottomed minger.

Before you present your exit face, keep in mind that interviewers are often nice at the end because they know they're seeing the back of you for ever, or sometimes cold because they want a final think before offering you the job. If you're too paranoid you could end on a glum face with that kind of resigned expression that says: 'Okay, we both know I haven't got it.' This could – in an extreme case – lose you the job.

Take your lead to leave from your interviewers. They should be experienced enough to display both verbal and non-verbal clues like moving their chair back a little and saying something like 'Well, if there are no more questions...' When this happens:

- Never leap out of your chair like a scalded cat. Not only does it make you look as though you're relieved the interview's over, it also makes you more clumsy. Exiting an interview room is a prime time for clumsy behaviour and speech. Ever found yourself saying something really stupid on the way out of a meeting? Unfortunately the brain has a habit of getting out of the room before your body does. Take your time and move carefully. You don't want to knock your chair over or hit your head on the door or screw up the goodbye handshake. Plan your exit just as carefully as you plan your entrance.
- Be prepared to shake hands again, so don't pick up any bags or papers in your right hand.

- Wait to see who offers you their hand. It's easy to shake too early, doing the full handshake ritual with someone who then says, 'Actually, I'm going to walk you to the reception.' Good interviewers should see you off the premises.
- Or they might leave you at the lift. If so, that's where you shake hands. This means coordinating it with the arrival of the lift. Expect them to wait for the lift to arrive, so shake just as you're about to get in.
- Don't forget your eye contact and smile ritual as you leave them. This isn't the time to suddenly find the floor a very attractive thing to look at.
- If you need a taxi it's okay to ask, but never ask the way to the nearest station or you'll look immature.
- Say thank you to the receptionist as you walk out.

Second Interviews

Never leave an interview with the thought that you'll never be called upon for a repeat performance. Second or even third interviews or call-backs are common in the business world and can be challenging if you made no real note of your original performance.

Interviewers don't just want to see you again to check through new details or information, they sometimes want to see that you are image-consistent. For this purpose you'll need to keep a memory or even a note of your first interview, including answers to questions and how you marketed yourself.

Did you look keen or cool? How did you describe your strengths and weaknesses? Being word or even body language perfect might look suspicious but so will bouncing in grinning if you were formal and straight-faced in the first interview.

Bigger Productions

Of course most of these tips have focused on the very simplest style of interview, but modern businesses often like to turn the recruitment interview into a bit of an epic. You could be interviewed by a large panel, in which case do remember to use eye contact on all of them, having first addressed your answer to the person who asked it. Some panel members might not appear to participate very much but that's no reason to ignore them.

Your interview could involve call-backs, walk-the-jobs and a mini-induction. Sometimes any or all of these visits can seem relaxed and informal but please don't be fooled – whenever you're on the premises you're being monitored. I've seen candidates get through the formal interview stage but let themselves down by cracking jokes and larking around on a walk-the-job or displaying a lack of basic manners when they're eating in the canteen during lunch.

Key occasions like recruitment interviews call for effort and planning. Think how much depends on your performance and then decide how much time you feel you can donate to helping yourself succeed. Be like an actor going out on stage: don't just rehearse and memorise your lines but work on your appearance, posture and movements as well.

Key Points:

- Prepare your performance beforehand – avoid advice to 'just be yourself'.
- Your two key moments are your entrance and your exit.
- Use eye contact on everyone present.
- Create a small thinking pause before you answer each question.
- Mirror their overall pace and body language 'tone'.

12

BODYTALK IN THE WORKPLACE

There's really no denying the effect your body language techniques will have in the workplace. As businesses get bigger and communications less personal, the cult of 'dead communication' is rife. Sadly electronic dependence plus a whole raft of politically correct rules and a terror of litigation has knocked the stuffing out of business in terms of individualism and personality. It does sometimes seem that really charismatic leaders, people willing to take risks to be brilliant, or people who can inspire, motivate, amuse or entertain by force of personality alone are as rare as hen's teeth, particularly in the bigger companies. I visit many workplaces in the space of a year and not only is it hard to tell one from another in terms of image and culture – no matter what their business is – it's also increasingly difficult to tell the employees apart. I suffer from déjà vu when I visit, most often when I go to a company that I've never been in before. The people look and act the same; there are the same jobs and the same roles, and the same spouting of business terms and jargon.

I'm not saying the people I meet are boring, it's just that today's workplace environment has cast a patina of dullness over everything. Even media offices like magazines and newspapers have been made grey, sterile wastelands. It's as though we're being asked to take our personalities and bury them somewhere inside ourselves while we sit staring at screens all day. Colour, texture, noise, expressed anger or excitement or pleasure have all been sucked away and no one seems to have noticed.

Years ago an 'office job' was just one of many career options, but thanks to the computer we're all office workers now. Your doctor sits staring blankly at her screen while you recite your medical problems and she will probably point you in the direction of a website to get more information on your illness. Plumbers visit clutching a laptop. The police spend more time logging info into their computers than they do chasing crime, and even home-workers like myself end up sitting in front of a grey- or beige-framed screen with a cursor beating like a robotic pulse.

We've become a world of backs of heads. Once it only used to be taxi drivers who would ask me to analyse their body language, despite the fact that I could only see half a skull from the back seat. Now I walk into open-plan offices and get asked 'What did you think of them?' when all I am looking at is a sea of hunched shoulders and backs of heads.

This part of the book is all about bringing personal qualities like charisma and charm back into the workplace. Why is this so important? What's the immediate benefit to you of indulging in a charisma offensive?

- Because the ability to have impact and influence and to persuade, inspire and motivate will increase your work effectiveness by 100 per cent.
- Because you will be creating and defining your own workplace image rather than letting other people perceive

you in a random way that has more to do with feedback, assumptions, whispered discussions and misunderstandings than real skills, abilities and talent.

- Because we've all been in or seen a situation where someone with talent has been passed over for promotion because they have been judged by the way they look and behave in their current role rather than having their potential for responsibility, status and leadership recognised.
- Because business is always very time-poor and if you don't make an effect straight away you may not get another chance.

I'm aware that time poverty affects your working life too. Because you're busy, I've used as many lists and bullet points as I can to make sure there are valuable tips you can read at a glance. We've all picked up business self-help books that are so long-winded you know from page one you'll never make the time or even work up the motivation to get through them. So this rant of an introduction is as wordy as I'm going to get. And if you like your mission statements, here's one I prepared earlier to describe all the things that will benefit you from the following section:

- This chapter will boost your impact, raise your profile and help sell you in ways you've never been sold before.
- You'll be shown how to make the best impression with the least effort.
- You'll learn how to sell, motivate, persuade and influence, mingle and network.
- You'll know how to do business presentations and business meetings.
- And how to lead or manage.

- There will also be techniques for front-line staff to help provide genuine customer care that works.

So, get stuck in. Pick out the bits you need or read through the whole lot; either way it will only take a few moments but could transform your whole life!

BODY LANGUAGE TYPES

Psychometric testing is still very hot in the business world. If you haven't been 'done' yet, all you need to know is that it normally takes the form of a series of questions that you answer about yourself, and which are repeated so often that it's very difficult to lie. Your answers are then correlated and you are placed into a behaviour category. There are usually three or four categories and you will then be told how you will behave in most scenarios.

I've created a similar form of typecasting for your body language. While stereotyping is usually a bad thing, this identification of your own style of bodytalk will be valuable because it will enable you to flex it when you want to communicate effectively with others. In the workplace it's this flexing that will become one of your greatest tools for persuading and influencing.

First you need to discover your current style of bodytalk. Then you can learn to identify other styles and see how to lock into them to be more effective with the person you're meeting. This is a very powerful tool but, like every other tip in this book, it requires subtlety and practice. If you're caught out changing your style too obviously you could come across as desperately insincere.

Are you a Mover, Performer, Empathist or Analyst? Read through the following profiles and see if your face fits.

You're a Mover if...

You tend to be clear and concise when you speak, with a dislike of waffle or small talk. You're driven and competitive and like to take charge of tasks and situations. Your body language is high in impact and energy with very little waste.

Signature gestures

- Strong, sustained bouts of eye contact that can become staring
- Looking for an exit when you get bored
- Upright posture
- Arms folded if you get bored
- Leaning forward
- Frowning
- Pointing and other directive gestures
- Emphatic gestures
- Tapping (when you want to move things on)
- Pacing

You're a Performer if...

You like being the centre of attention and tend to use humour a lot in your workplace communications. However, you have a short attention span and get bored easily.

You have an enthusiastic style, preferring gut reactions to research and detail. You're better at talking than listening and you love new things and ideas.

Signature gestures

- Expressive facial expressions
- Often smiling or laughing
- Speedy movements
- Can't keep still for long
- Can't speak without using your hands
- Open, dramatic gestures
- Illustrative gestures

You're an Empathist if...

You place a lot of importance on relationships at work and like to know what makes people tick. Small talk and other more personal conversations are vital to you. You're not someone who craves the glory or limelight, preferring to influence via coaching or motivating. You use a lot of inclusive techniques, encouraging other people to speak and share their views.

Signature gestures

- Smiling
- Nodding
- Leaning forward to listen
- Sitting rather than standing
- Friendly touch
- Mirroring
- Low-key hand gestures
- Intense listening
- Self-hugs
- Body barrier gestures

You're an Analyst if...

You're happy working alone for long periods of time. You enjoy planning, research and logical thinking. You tend to be quiet and have an eye for detail, spotting small errors as well as bigger mistakes or problems in a project. You like to talk quietly, using logic and research to back up your thoughts. You prefer to take time to make decisions about new ideas. You're a starter and a finisher. Once you begin a project you will always see it through to the very end.

Signature gestures
- Facing your screen and working while you talk
- Low-key gestures
- Ability to use eye contact to make your point
- Frequent use of exclusive gestures, making you look lost in your own thoughts at times, rather than communicating externally

How to Persuade and Influence

Once you've identified your profile, you can learn to spot the style of anyone you're talking to, even in very speedy transactions. Look for clues about the way they work or the way your meeting was booked. Were they thorough and was it well planned or was it more on the hoof, with interruptions? Do they like to make small talk at the start or get straight down to business? How are their listening skills? How quickly do they talk and how animated are they?

Keep an open mind but start to hunt for clues as soon as you're introduced. Your next step is to create what's called a complementary transaction style.

Like doesn't always appreciate like, and Performers and Analysts, and Movers and Empathists will probably have the biggest struggle creating fast-track rapport and empathy. This is

THE BODY LANGUAGE BIBLE

the core problem with business transactions, as opposed to social ones. In business you might only get a few moments with your audience. Maybe you deal with the public or maybe you work in a busy company where conversations are fleeting. You might have a boss or chief executive who only puts in sporadic appearances, and who you have to impress quickly or risk losing the moment. Modern business often has a feeling of speed-dating about it!

Opposites Attract

Let's start with some negatives. Movers can struggle to enjoy their transactions with Empathists. When the Empathist wants to stand and chat over coffee and biscuits, the Movers want to make quick points and move on. Movers are not hugely interested in feelings or emotions. They're time-driven and consider the Empathists too touchy-feely. At times they're exasperated by them. Empathists, on the other hand, can consider Movers aggressive and borderline rude.

Analysts, on the other hand, can find the Performer a complete waste of space. Always cracking jokes and not being fully researched or in touch with logical fact and reasoning, the Performer will find that his or her normal charm offensive cuts no ice with the Analyst, who values hard facts and evidence over entertainment and gut reaction any day of the week. In reverse, the Performer can find the Analyst dour and boring, a bucket of cold water thrown over all their enthusiasm and creative ideas.

So will like-meets-like be a match made in heaven? Not necessarily.

- Two Movers could get into a competition for power or status that turns into a fight to the death.

232

- Two Performers might amuse one another initially, but they could also find themselves vying for the spotlight.
- Two Empathists could have more instant rapport with one another as they share an enjoyment of chatting and listening.
- Two Analysts *should* work together in calm harmony.

To create the rapport that will enable you to be persuasive and influential over someone else at work you'll need to take two vital steps:

1 **Know yourself**

   This means having an effective assessment of your own profile or communication and bodytalk styles right now, today. I've described a profile of each type but of course you'll identify more strongly with some of their qualities than others. For instance, you might be a Mover who can enjoy some amount of small talk, or an Analyst who likes to socialise now and again. Keeping the types in mind, create your own profile, making it as accurate as possible.

2 **Tailor your style**

   The second step is to spot the profile or type of person you want to be more effective with. Once you've done that, you need to plan out how to be complementary to their communication style and tailor your own accordingly.

To influence a Mover
- Plan your communications and make sure they're well structured before you get into conversation.
- Keep it concise.
- Use emphatic but not challenging body language. Avoid

higher-status displays as otherwise Movers will never agree with your idea or point, just want to smash you down to a lower status level.

- Be prepared to use submissive displays on occasion to score a 'hit' but only when you can see their decisions will be based on bigging themselves up.
- Make sure your gestures are congruent with your speech. Movers have a nose for people who are trying it on or who don't know what they're talking about.
- Stand face-on and use eye contact.
- Never pin the Mover down; they like an escape route.
- Sell them ideas that will make them feel like a winner, or that will allow them to take personal glory.

To influence a Performer

- Laugh at their jokes.
- Display energy, enthusiasm and positivity.
- Use open gestures that veer on the side of expansive and dramatic.
- Never fold your arms or look away.
- Never shake your head or look negative.
- Offer to relieve them of some of the detail or paperwork.
- Applaud them when possible; they love a clap. Big applause if they've performed at a lecture, but even one small impulsive-looking clap of your hands will impress them at smaller gatherings.
- Smile a lot.

To influence an Empathist

- Drop everything and display active listening signals.
- Always accept tea or coffee or food if it's offered.

- Look at them, not the door.
- Use touch when appropriate.
- Sit quite close to speak.
- Use open gestures that display palms.
- If you allow body language 'leakage', understand they will be the type most likely to pick up on your true feelings.
- Smile – but make it genuine, nothing overcongruent.
- Don't interrupt or rush an Empathist.

To influence an Analyst

- Tone down your body language. Analysts will only be persuaded by facts and logic.
- Use a calm voice and calm gestures. Coordinated, smooth emphatic gestures that aren't overcongruent should work.
- Avoid touch.
- Avoid too much eye contact. Reflective eye gaze will impress them more, as will pausing before answering questions.
- A small frown will impress.
- Folded arms are fine, especially while you're thinking.
- Avoid 'hurry' gestures, like looking at your watch or tapping.

CHARISMA FOR BEGINNERS

It's so easy to be charismatic at work that I always wonder why more people don't try it. For a start there's so little competition or comparison that you'll probably have a clear run at it. Sometimes even smiling or using eye contact will make you stand out from the herd. By upping your charisma by as little as 5 per cent you'll probably be streets ahead. Read this then and you'll clean up.

By the way, I'm not suggesting for one minute that you shouldn't be good at your job. All these charismatic techniques are intended to sit on top of your talent like advertising and marketing sits on top of a good product. It's just that I meet a lot of people in the workplace who have shedloads of talent but never achieve recognition, plus a lot of people who are struggling, conscientious and hard-working who also never really obtain greatness. The point is you need to market yourself.

What is Charisma?

Like stress and good sex we all know what we mean by charisma and yet it's hard to define it. If I asked you to make a list of charismatic people you'd probably start with Nelson Mandela and Bill Clinton and then stall. So what is charisma and how can you get it?

I don't normally like plundering dictionaries when I run courses or write books as they often don't take account of word perception, by which I mean the generally understood meaning of words, and perception is what I'm all about. However it's useful to know what we should mean when we refer to charisma: 'an extraordinary power in a person, group, cause... which takes hold of popular imagination, wins popular support...' (*Longman Modern English Dictionary*).

The good news is that charisma doesn't have to be part of your DNA. You can't buy it in a shop but you sure can learn it and develop the techniques. The other good thing is that they're quite simple and easy to put into practice. What's the bad news? There isn't any really, it's all good.

Keeping it Simple

There's a lot of complicated nonsense out there claiming to be advice about making an impression at work, but ignore all that. Sometimes magic is easy. So here's rule number one:

Rule 1: stick to simple tricks

I know you've been told that 'no pain equals no gain' but I promise you it's not true in this case. By creating simple goals and steps for yourself and then sticking to them you'll make the most dramatic changes. Here are three for you to be going on with:

1 Always make a great entrance
2 Learn to smile
3 Learn to shake hands

Easy? Of course. But look around at other people you work with: how many of them manage to achieve and perform these three most basic traits of the charismatic personality? How many of your colleagues drift into the office or into meeting rooms looking like zombies and spend the first few precious first-impression minutes moaning about how tired they are? How many of them are diffident or ignorant about the basic techniques of shaking someone's hand? How many of them dogface or do screensaver facial expressions when they meet clients as well as other colleagues? Well you're not going to be one of them.

Rule 2: project and absorb in equal measure

Learn how to network. The charismatic profile means wearing an appearance of inner balance and harmony that will count as confidence, but make sure it never looks like self-absorption. You will need to appear comfortable in your own skin rather than in love with yourself. Vanity and smugness aren't marketable qualities in the UK, but looking as though you know what you're doing is.

Beware looking like you are your own prime concern though. Charismatic people *absorb*, paying attention to other people, noticing other people and listening to other people. This isn't just ear-listening, either. It barely matters that you're hanging on their every word if you *look* distracted or bored. Here's a quick test to see how good or bad your projecting and absorption skills are:

- Did you choose a desk facing the door to the office or room you work in? Or do you have your back to the main thoroughfare or entrance? (I know it's not always possible to choose where you sit at work, therefore if you were given the option which would you pick?)
- Do you ever get out of your seat to greet visitors, no matter what their status?
- Do you ever carry on working when people are talking to you, even if it's just a few words on the keyboard and you know you're not missing anything they say?
- Do you ever interrupt people when they're speaking to you?
- When you're in a meeting do you pride yourself on being able to float in and out of the proceedings, working on a need-to-know basis?
- Do you find people often repeat things they've already said?
- Do you ever sit with your chin in your hand at meetings?
- Do you find it easier to concentrate if you look out of the window?
- Are you an avid multi-tasker, making sure you get chores done while you're taking a phone call?
- Do you usually eat or drink during meetings and enjoy power lunches where you discuss business?

I'm sure you can see from your answers just how much half-baked listening you're doing. When did you last give someone the luxury of your undivided attention? Here are some questions about your self-absorption signals:

- When someone's speaking to you are you partly listening but mainly formulating your response or working out what it is you want to say next?
- Do you find it easy to change the subject during a discussion?
- When someone else speaks do you often find yourself picking, fiddling or tapping your pen?
- Do you ever ask a question just so that it will have to be asked of you, as in 'What's your favourite film then?'
- Are you comfortable telling other people about your likes and dislikes?
- Do you use the word 'I' a lot when you speak?
- Do you ever talk about yourself in the third person, as in: 'I'm just being myself, this is what Judi James is like'?

Projection is vital for your workplace charisma, and being and acting invisible just shouldn't be an option. But you do need to go one step further. As well as drawing yourself out, make sure you learn to draw others out too. Charismatic people don't big themselves up; they do it to others, making people around them feel important and valued.

Rule 3: get the status signals right

All businesses are hierarchical. Your place in that hierarchy will depend on three key things:

1 **Your anointed status**

   This comes along with the job title. You might be called 'manager' or 'MD' or 'team leader' and other workers will be aware you're in charge.

2 **Your animal status**

   This is your genuine place in the pecking order. It will be decided by the amount of respect your colleagues have for you and your abilities.

3 **Your mean status**

   There are certain individuals in any company who define their own status according to the amount of fake or psychological power they can wield. If you've seen the US comedy series *Scrubs* you'll know the janitor who is able to bully the doctors by his knowledge of the building. Businesses are full of similar bullies, usually working for IT or accounts. Their anointed status is low (often being seen as 'support') but their niche knowledge means they're able to flex their power muscles, often as acts of revenge.

To be successful in business – or even to get a job in the first place – you will need to play those power signals like a Stradivarius.

Rule 4: put in a good performance

There is no such thing as 'being yourself' at work. (Unless you work from home and never use the phone. Even then I'll bet you still have to get out there and perform when you plug whatever product you've been hatching.) Actors recognise their key performance moments and train for them, rehearse for them and research for them. They get their bodies and minds into shape and they work towards their success. Why are business people so lacklustre about their performance prep time? A common excuse is that 'I didn't have time to prepare for that presentation or meeting.' What do you think an actor would do if he was told to go out on stage with no time to prepare for or learn the part? Would he wander in front of the audience, blink into the spotlights and apologise for being nervous and having no idea about the script? No, they would freak.

Your key performance moments at work will be these:

- *Academy Award-winners*
  This is when you address a group of shareholders, do a business presentation, speak at a conference or address that big board meeting.
- *Starring roles*
  These performances are the recruitment or promotion interviews, one-to-ones, meetings, customer meetings, running training or inductions, front-line customer trans-actions or complaint handling.
- *Supporting roles*
  Team-building, training or away days or talking business to colleagues.
- *Walk-ons*
  Any other appearances that appear more passive, like arriving at work, sitting at your desk, leaving, eating lunch, etc.

Recognise the fact that you're performing, just as an actor performs on stage. If you're in denial ('It's just a quick chat/small presentation' 'I didn't really know what I was talking about' 'Someone asked me to do it') you really do need to grow up quickly because that is unprofessional thinking and behaviour, and won't help with your charisma rating.

A Tell-Free Zone

Please remember what I said on previous pages, that self-marketing is not about 'tell'. Although you should make it a rule to never talk yourself down, bigging yourself up verbally sounds shallow and desperate. I was once monitoring a *Big Brother* housemate whose cries of 'I'm a really nice girl' and 'I don't normally moan like this, I'm normally fun!' were getting louder and more frequent just as her behaviour was getting so unpleasant that everyone began to dislike her.

'Show' is the thing, then. Remember one of the core learning phrases in this book is 'show, don't tell', and like all charismatic people you're going to show everyone just how good you are via the medium of body language.

The behaviours you're about to learn are not 'pick and mix'. Once you start doing them you're going to do them all the time, but that's okay because doing them all the time will make them easier whereas turning them on and off will make them a performance that will be hard to make look congruent.

The Good, the Bad and the Ugly

There are no absolute body language 'rights' or 'wrongs' although in the workplace it's especially useful to carry a quick mental checklist of do's and don'ts, so here are some visual images that should flash into your mind when you need an instant check-up:

Making a great entrance
Good
Walking in with your body completely visible, pulled up

straight, hands free or bag in left hand, eye contact to front, offering a confident smile of greeting.

Bad

Looking at door-handle, right hand carrying bag. Never walk in looking self-obsessed. Your attention should be undivided and focused on the people in the room.

Poking head round door. Never walk into a room looking guilty or low-status.

Juggling food or drinks. Carry as little as possible, you'll need your hands for meeting and greeting. Never arrive at work or a meeting clutching your breakfast.

Shaking hands

Good

Standing face-to-face, smiling, eye contact, elbows bent, hands around waist-height. Use undivided attention techniques, facing full-on where possible.

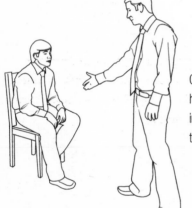

Guest sitting, host approaching with hand extended, smiling. Use an intentional gesture to allow your visitor time to stand before you shake.

Bad

Shaking hands over a desk, half-crouched. Never lean across a desk to shake hands.

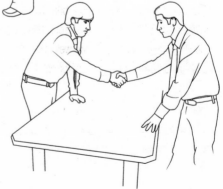

One person grabbing the other's arm as they shake. Never use a handshake to capture your victim.

Never use a handshake as an opportunity to power-posture. An example would be when the shaker takes the visitor's hand to shake but uses it to pull them in to hug. Avoid a forced acceleration of affection. It should be mutual.

Standing
Good

Feet about shoulder-width apart, body straight but relaxed, hands lightly clasped in front. This describes the Power Pose, where you are well planted and well balanced, hands ready for emphatic gestures.

Half-perched on table or desk, one leg bent, one cheek on table, arms loose on lap. This is called a half-sit, still active enough to be a standing pose and dominate attention but very relaxed.

Bad

Legs splayed too wide, arms folded. This is aggressive alpha-signalling, like a nightclub bouncer.

Legs crossed while standing – the passive scissors pose.

Feet slightly apart, toes slightly pointed together, ankles bent outward. This is a passive, juvenile stance signalling compliance.

- Standing with your legs almost together and your arms straight down by your sides. This stance is too unnatural and android.
- Standing with a slumped posture. This is weak and compliant, and signals that you are low energy and not worth listening to.
- Standing with your hands clasped behind your back, legs apart. This stance, most usually performed by men, has an air of enforced authority.
- Standing holding your coffee high up on your chest, near your chin. This barrier suggests you'd rather be left alone.
- Standing with your legs slightly splayed, hands covering crotch. This is the defensive fig-leaf pose that suggests you feel under attack.

Sitting

Good

- Legs crossed, elbows propped on arms of chair, hands loosely clutched in lap.
- Legs uncrossed, knees slightly apart, elbows on arms of chair, hands loosely clasped (this is only a good sitting position for men).
- Sitting forward in the chair, legs slightly splayed, elbows on thighs, you'll look keen to listen, but be careful of being overcongruent – you risk looking too keen.
- Legs crossed, one elbow over back of chair, hands lightly clasped. This makes you look confident as long as the chair-back is the right height and shape to pull the pose off smoothly. You could risk looking slightly disconnected from the discussion though.

Bad

- Legs splayed wide, arms folded tight on chest, slightly slumped. The position gives off mixed signals: a strongly dominant or arrogant crotch display combined with guarded body barrier that makes you look argumentative and stubborn.
- Arms and legs crossed. This signifies closed to attempts at communication.
- Arms behind head, legs splayed. This is the classic pit-baring pose that exposes all your most delicate body parts, making you look arrogant.
- Arms clasped behind chair, legs wrapped around chair legs. You look as though you're being held hostage.
- Perching on edge of chair, tucked into the side or corner of the room. This makes you look nervous and anxious.

- Slumped and looking down. You'll come across as negative and bored.

- Straddling back of chair. Here you'll seem playful, gungho, flirty but totally obnoxious.

- One leg across the other, calf on top of thigh. This is not an especially negative pose but still a form of barrier, making you appear disconnected or judgemental.

- Same leg position as previously but torso leaning back slightly and hands on calf. This hand gesture reinforces the barrier nature of the pose, making you look like you're not in agreement with what's being said.

- Sitting upright with steepled fingers, elbows resting on arms of chair. This pose appears to emphasise your status to the point where it demeans that of the person with you.

- Legs splayed wide, elbows hooked over the back of the chair. This pose is aggressive and combative.

- Sitting on top of one leg, which is crooked under your bottom. This suggests you're instinctive, childlike and energetic plus quite keen to raise your status by raising your height.

- Legs crossed on the chair. This pose suggests you're either completely childlike or that you have spiritual tendencies.

Your Manipulative Body Language Techniques

In the 80s, budding salesmen and entrepreneurs were taught how to take control of meetings with powerful body language techniques. These included gems like the power shake, where they fought to get their hand on top in the shake, and the eye-stare, where you engaged your victim in an eye-contact stand-off with the loser being the one who looked away first. These are now quite rightly deemed corny and too much like testosterone-fuelled posturing to have a place in modern life. However there are subtler bonding and influencing techniques you can use to get better results from any meeting, conversation or transaction and I've listed them below.

Warning: It's very easy to get overexcited at the thought of using subliminal bonding techniques but *don't*! These tips are to be used subtly; the minute you exaggerate them you get shown a yellow card for crassness above and beyond the call of duty. Now before I let you in on a few trade secrets repeat after me: 'I must remember to be subtle...I must remember to be subtle...I must remember to be subtle...'

- **Postural echo, postural congruence or mirroring**
  Like-bodied tends to look like-minded so when in doubt just pick up on your partner or fellow speaker's body posture and pace and copy it. What you're doing is mimicking the natural behaviour of close friends who will automatically mimic one another when they meet or are in conversation. If you like someone you try to *be* like them, too. This technique is called postural echo, mirroring or mimicry. It's a bit like walking up to someone who's already dancing and joining in with them. You match the pace of their movement and their overall position and mood. To get this right you need to be subtle, though. What you don't do is create a perfect mirror image because they'll think you're taking the mickey. Do work on this before you use it. It's good to rehearse with a friend and get him or her to let you know when your mirroring is becoming too obvious.
- **Pacing and leading**
  This is über-powerful stuff that also requires a light and

deft touch to make it effective. You talk with someone who is in a state that you find unproductive. Either they are too shy or closed or they appear nervous or too anxious. You begin by slightly mirroring their pose and/or energy. Then as you speak with them you begin to move your own body language into the state you want them to be in. This means beginning to open out if you started with your arms folded in a barrier or slowly calming down if you began by mirroring their jittery nerves, anger or anxiety. By gradually altering your own state, having started from theirs, you should be able to lead them to the same state you end in. Again, practise this one in a safe environment because it's hard to do consciously.

- **Transfix**
  When your customer goes off the point or keeps trying to change the subject you can use a transfix to get them back to the point. This is where your body language pose holds when you've been interrupted to show a desire to get back to your point when they've finished.

- **Intentional gestures or announcements**
  These gestures tend to mime a partial movement, like slightly raising your hand when you want to speak at a meeting, sitting slightly forward when you want to interrupt; alerting signals, where you use an eye-flash (quick, meaningful glance), take off spectacles or clear your throat, etc., or even body guides, where you pat or touch someone subtly to steer them.

- **Back-channel signals**
  These are subtle ways of steering a conversation via nodding to encourage or changing your pace or looking around a room to end a conversation and signal a desire to move on.

Unpopularity at work

There are two easy ways to make yourself unpopular at work: one is to be the boss and spend every waking moment reminding your colleagues of that fact, and the second is to *not* be the boss, but keep throwing your weight around as though you were.

In power and status terms here are a few other options. Do you see yourself in one of these categories? If so, it's a good idea to look at your body language and see what you can change to improve your status:

- Reflectors – people who hang around the boss, brown-nosing, or people who embark on sexual relationships with the boss to bask in the reflected glory.
- Dippers – people who adopt high or low status signals depending on the circumstances.
- Hiders – people who yearn for status but who fail to display status signals then complain when they get looked over for promotion, claiming the boss should have spotted the fact that they were capable of change if and when the promotion had been offered.
- Skulkers – people who prefer to be submissive.

Overkill high-status signals in the workplace

If you're genuinely high-status and comfortable with that you shouldn't need to throw your weight around verbally or visually. These following signals come under the heading of Power Posturing. Genuinely high-status people will usually have the confidence to avoid these at all times.

- Standing too close
- Standing behind someone
- Power-shaking (keeping your hand on top in the handshake)

- Shake and grab – using an arm-clench to control the other person as you shake
- Shake-and-pat, patting the other person as you shake their hand
- Power-patting – patting the other person on the back or shoulder
- Using more space than everyone else
- Sitting or standing higher than everyone
- Chin raised, looking down your nose
- Not smiling back or acknowledging someone when they greet you
- Wide-splayed legs
- Hands on hips
- Chest stuck out
- Pit-baring
- Smug smile
- Staring
- Frowning
- Metronomic gestures
- Steepled fingers
- Cut-off signals, closing your eyes when someone is talking to you or you're talking to them
- Aggressive arm-fold
- Looking more relaxed than the other person
- Stomping in high heels
- Steering other people

Low-status signals

There are times in business when you should choose to lower your own status to accommodate a guest, client or higher-ranking workmate. However, you should avoid overkill on low-status gestures just as much as you should avoid Power Posturing.

While some subtle body-lowering, smiling or mirroring can be appropriate, the following gestures will do you no favours at all:

- Giggling, over-smiling or adding a small laugh at the end of everything you say
- Crouching or hunching
- Making your body look smaller, pulling your arms into your sides, etc.
- Tottering in high heels
- Using less space than others
- Arm or hand barriers
- Stuffing your hands in your pockets
- Face-touching or face-covering
- Hand-rubbing
- Fiddling, looking self-absorbed
- Lack of eye contact
- A dipped head
- Allowing yourself to be led
- A weak handshake
- A hand that is snatched away too soon
- Neck-touching or holding
- Nail-biting
- Sitting or standing with legs or torso turned partially away
- Legs and arms crossed
- Sitting on the edge of the seat
- Sitting with feet either pointing towards or heading towards the door
- Palms-up gesture
- Tip-toeing into meetings
- Always sitting at the back

Status spats are unseemly and you should never get suckered in. However, it's important to remember that continually lying down and rolling over will only get you labelled – quite rightly – as a wuss. The challenge then is to exude confidence, reliability, wisdom and natural authority without upsetting your colleagues.

What this means is spraying your territory with that quality we've mentioned throughout this chapter:

CHARISMA

Quick Tips for Business Charisma
Start your positive performance before you get to the building

Always arrive 10–15 minutes early and park yourself in a café to get yourself focused and into your ideal 'state'. Never start your day at your desk. Always arrive ready to hit the ground running. Otherwise you're like an actor getting into costume and slap on stage. By correcting your body language message before you get to the entrance you'll feel like less of a sham. Pull yourself up into your Power Walk. Adjust your rate of stride. The sound of your feet plus your aura of energy will impress or depress other colleagues on a subconscious level. Too fast will appear stressed, especially if you take small, clacking strides. Too slow looks depressed and reluctant. To appear charismatic you need to appear ready to face each day and each situation with energy and enthusiasm, not terror, boredom or reluctance.

- *How not to leak:*
  Any subliminal signals of dissent from your own body will destroy your overall message. Power Walking will be scuppered if you show it's an act. Your biggest risks of leakage will come from: clenched teeth, being seen taking

a deep breath, and a vocal tone that is too high, bright and chippy. You're not an air hostess serving drinks as the plane goes down. Drop the tone from 'breezy' to 'friendly' and try to walk in a way that makes less foot-noise. It's amazing how fast cloppy feet send out a message of 'I know we're all suffering here and I'm suffering more than most but if I can look bright then so can you lot.' Your body language should never look reproachful to others. Make it your aim to raise their mood but not by scolding. We've all heard the 'good morning' through clenched teeth. Avoid the sigh, too!

Affect, don't be affected

The first few people you see when you walk into your work-place are not responsible for your mood for the rest of the day. Some receptionists and security guards are not fresh from charm school and many make it their life's work to take out their own inadequacies on the rest of the world. Always go into 'holding' mode with your body language. Keep your facial expression polite and friendly. Other people's moods are of no interest to your body language performance. Find out their name and greet them by using it. Never stop to talk though. There is a law of human dynamics that states the more miserable and rude front-line staff are, the harder employees try to cheer them up. Don't. It's a waste of effort. Employ holding mode and move on.

- *How not to leak:*
  Never show impatience or anxiety gestures en route to your desk. Looking at your watch as you wait in the queue for reception will only let everyone know you're late, also that you have a lower-status job where arrival time

matters. Never complain about the weather with your face. Pretend in your head that you love every season and walk in wearing that expression. Never use moaning as a bonding device. Your key body language leakage points here could be: a sour expression on your face, shoulders raised upward through stress of journey, queuing at reception like a caged animal, pacing and eyes scanning about for escape, ditto at the lift, using lift or reception time to start work by phoning or texting or opening your laptop. This will let everyone know you're badly organised. Never be seen doing work outside of your workspace, it's bad PR.

Lifts matter

Every part of your workplace should be seen as a networking opportunity. I don't mean you should be asking for a pay rise in the lift, but you should be projecting yourself in a positive light at every location. I was recently working in a radio studio when a woman walked past, stomping along with an unsmiling facial expression. 'Fancy working with her!' a woman beside me said. Her companion nodded. Both were series producers and radio is a very small world. You never know who you'll be impressing or not. Err on the side of caution; after all it costs nothing to smile. Never be affected by the overall culture of your company. It matters not if no one else does smiling and greeting in the corridor, lift or offices. Do it and keep doing it. In fact it will work in your favour if the place is overall gloomy as it will make your relentless charm offensive even more noticeable.

- *How not to leak:*
  You will possibly find networking embarrassing at first. After all, it might be groundbreaking work. If so, avoid the

pause. The pause is that moment when you first see someone when you try to decide whether to greet them or not, or try to summon up the courage to do so. Pauses don't work, though. No one ever mustered courage by use of a pause. Pauses only drain your resolve. A pause is like an open door to your negative inner dialogues or NIDs. You'll start making up reasons and excuses for not saying hello. Don't pause, just do it.

Seating plans matter

Space and your use of it is a vital part of your workplace success. Space and territory are what wars are fought over and you should never underestimate the importance of either.

- Move to the sides of the lift when someone new arrives but don't self-bunch. If there is a rail, spread your arms out slightly along it.
- When possible never take a desk with your back to the door of the office. It makes you vulnerable in animal terms and will affect your mood and sense of well-being. It also makes you look like an automaton to anyone walking in. You should always sit where you can see newcomers just by flicking up your eyes.
- In an oblong office fight to get the desk up and towards the right from the door. Left is friendly but right is powerful. You can do friendly with your facial expression.
- Keep your desk tidy. Mess creates cluttered thinking and looks like nesting which looks like set views and boring thoughts. Energise your desk space. Never sit surrounded by things from the past like old paperwork, awards, previous projects or old pens, plants or coffee cups. Business is

forward-thinking and in a permanent state of change and that's how you should look. The only personal things on your desk should be a photo of someone or something you like, like pets, kids or your house, to the left of your screen and an idealised shot of the team you work in on the right, to promote more positive feeling about them when the going gets tough. When they look at your desk it will also make it look as though you care, too.

- Make your desk 'poser-friendly'. Check the height of your chair to ensure your legs are supported but not dangling. Adjust the back support so that you can sit straight for long periods of time rather than slumping. Clear out any junk or other matter from beneath your desk so that you have lots of room for your legs and feet to stretch out. Have your screen tilted and at the right height so your eyes are about level with the top line. Have a wrist support in front of your keyboard. If you're right-handed have your phone on the left-hand side of your desk so that you can pick up calls with your left hand and write with the right. Keep maximum space near your writing hand. Throw pens away when they break or run out of ink, don't just put them back in the tub. Make sure your phone wire isn't tangled or coiled or you'll drag everything across or off your desk every time you answer the phone.

- Never eat food at your desk. Do I need to explain this? It looks like you're doing a 'work-through', which will make it look as though you have too much work, which will make you look too non-assertive or stupid to say no. Or it will make you look like someone who eats where they sit like an animal who works and sits in its own trough. If you have a shred of self-respect get up and eat somewhere else. Better still, go out.

- Do good daydream body language. Your brain is primed to daydream every ninety minutes or so. Daydreaming is good because it reboots the brain. Bad daydream bodytalk is bad though because it looks as though you're doing nothing. It's vital to plan a good daydream position that works, then. I find raising my chin, gazing up and to the left with my chin cupped in the palm of my hand and my fingers tapping gently across my mouth is good. It tends to project the message that you're lost in deeper thought, not playing solitaire on your screen or gazing mindlessly at the screensaver.

- Try to hold meetings at a round table rather than at your desk. Sit up and to the right from the door.

- If the table is oblong or the typical board-table style you're into hierarchy city. There are two key power positions in this scenario, either the patriarch seat at the end of the table or the 'Last Supper' seat in the middle of the long side at the far side from the door. Only ever take these if you're in charge and want to press that point home. Never sit opposite anyone who is in either of these seats as it will make you look like a usurper. Never sit next to these seats as it will make you look like admin or a brown-noser or both. Try to sit opposite but angled slightly to the right. They'll see you as visible but they'll also see you as part of the future vision rather than the trusted old retainers. Work on what their view is, not your own. How often do we pick seats that make us feel comfortable or that make other people look better to us?

- If you're interviewing someone never use the old trick of

sitting at the corner of the table to avoid getting a barrier between you. This position is only suitable for a doctor/patient relationship as it implies touch and they'll think you're about to do a full rectal examination. Have a whole table between you rather than this.

Chairs matter

There are some seats that will never allow you to look charismatic and others that will make even the biggest geek look powerful and confident. I've watched countless politicians fall at the junior school hurdle when they've accepted a kiddie seat to get closer to the pupils for a photo-opportunity and only realised their mistake when it was too late. It can happen with adult chairs too. Gordon Brown is a big man and his team need to get more chair-demanding. During a recent evening TV interview his chair was so small he looked as though he was squatting on a bean-bag. I know you can't always pick your chairs at work but when you have options or even clout, why settle for the prat's chair when you can have one that makes you look graceful and confident?

- Avoid chairs without arms. To look charismatic you'll need some sort of shelf for your elbows.
- Avoid the traditional secretary chairs. Functional but low-status.
- Only get a chair with a very high back if you're tall. Otherwise you'll look like a small kid.
- Pick a chair that adjusts to you and the way you like to sit, not a chair that dominates.
- Make sure your chair is the right height for you. Your legs shouldn't be raised up off the seat nor should they be dangling.

- Avoid sofas and armchairs. Great for the home but in business they add years to your age by making your posture look too 'old folk's home'.
- Never use a squeaky chair.
- Never roll your chair around the office like a Dalek.
- Chairs that rock or rotate are good but only in performance mode. Too much rocking will look manic or psychotic. Side-to-side rolling can look like stress.
- Perching on tables is great because it sits you higher than everyone else and implies leadership and energy. However all this evaporates if the table is unable to take your weight.

Entrances matter

Every entrance you make must be good. In fact, better than good, it needs to be brilliant. Unforgettable for all the right reasons. I want you to focus on projecting an aura of special-ness. Imagine you're the star walking out on stage, then drop some of the signals of arrogance. Here's how to do that: adjust to your Power Pose, pulling yourself up and ironing out your facial expression. Apply a relaxed-looking smile. This shouldn't include teeth-baring though. Over-smiling can look aggressive if it's a stretched social smile but smiling too much, even if there's an appropriate amount of teeth on display, can easily look low-status and submissive. Breathe out and walk into the office or room as though keen to meet the people in there. You should always arrive in an aura of energy. Not panic or stress, just posi-tive energy, so walk at a pace to imply enthusiasm. Pause when you get inside the room and take everyone in with a sweep of your eyes. Greet anyone you walk past, even if they don't reply. If you can learn their names for the greeting, use those too.

Don't talk on your out-breath as it will sound like a sigh. Never moan about the weather or anything. Never look as though you think you might be in the wrong room. At a formal meeting greet people with enthusiasm, shaking them by the hand but using your extended hand as an announcement gesture as you approach them.

- Always dress well and look smart.
- Wear something a little different. Charismatic people often sport signature garments, like Richard Branson's lack of a tie when all around are tie-wearers. This shows individual thinking, a liking for change and original ideas but an intrinsic ability to make controversial decisions and stick to them.
- Keep your desk tidy even if all around you sit in squalor.
- Walk the job on a regular basis. Network your way through other departments. Raise your profile throughout the entire company. Press the flesh everywhere and introduce yourself wherever possible, rather than becoming departmentalised.
- Face people when you talk to them and use eye contact. Give everyone a few moments of undivided and undiluted attention.
- Never moan or use negative body language signals.
- Avoid denial gestures as you speak, like dismissive shrugging, hand-flapping, eye-rolling and mouth-shrugging.
- Avoid status-lowering signals like crouching, self-hugging, hand-wringing, apologetic hand-clasping, face-touching, fiddling or self-grooming.
- Use positive, friendly tie-signs, like the odd touch, glance, mirrored gesture or postural echo.

- Use space to manipulate. Proxemics is a powerful tool that you can use to leave a lasting impression. Maintain a polite social space (3–4 feet) at most times. Isolate yourself when it counts. Like José Mourinho an ability to sit alone hunkered down and deep in thought during moments of pressure on the entire group will make you appear strategic. Then get closer (about 2–3 feet) either to create bonding and intimacy when someone has a problem or when you want to intimidate subtly. (Sit on the arm of their chair, perch on their desk but always stay in front of them, never lurk behind. Only pick on bigger or stronger colleagues in this way; you don't want to look like a bully.)

- Never look desk-bound or nested. Charisma means projecting energy, not squatting at a desk staring at a screen. Where possible turn your chair at an angle out towards the room so you can still project. Use your computer as little as possible. In image terms it's not a power-tool, it's just a fancy typewriter. I know many top entrepreneurs who have no idea at all how to use them and no desire to use them.

- Ditto with boy-toys like the BlackBerry. I know it's a marvellous gadget and I know it costs a fair old wedge but the body language involved impresses no one. Holding a small device in your palm and tapping at it with a dinky, dolly-size pen makes you look like a kid playing with a Stylophone or a waiter taking an order.

- Never walk around the office empty-handed. Always have some papers tucked under your arm. This makes you look busy and important.

- Get up to greet people who walk towards your desk. This allows you to perch rather than being pinned to your seat. Never allow anyone to stand over you while you sit.

- Never stand outside smoking. This looks naff beyond belief. Giving up shows resolve and self-control.

Charismatic Body Language Tricks

- Standing and perching on the side/edge of your desk when someone approaches.
- Facing straight-on when both standing and talking, one arm across your body and one knuckle touching your chin.
- Bill Clinton-style intros: standing with two other men, hand on one guy's shoulder while introducing him to the second guy.
- Sitting at your desk but with your chair turned slightly out to the rest of the room.

Charismatic Don'ts

- Slump slightly at desk, staring at screen.
- Stand legs splayed, hands on hips.
- Stand talking, weight on one hip, hands clutched high in front of body.
- Lean back in chair, feet on desk, hands behind head.

Celebrity Charismatic 'Types'

Bill Clinton

A perfect example of chief-executive-style charismatic leadership signals. Clinton is at his charismatic best one-to-one where he uses intense listening signals like eye contact, undivided attention and postural echo to make the person he meets feel touched by something special.

Hillary Clinton

Since she's taken her own place in the political arena Hillary has abandoned the submissive female posturing and adopted military signals of charismatic leadership instead. She rarely carries a bag but stands upright with her arms down by her sides. When she speaks it's usually just her head moving. This gives the impression of confidence and emotional strength. Unlike her husband's signals these work best to large groups.

Princess Diana

Her charismatic signals came from a blend of a naturally regal bearing combined with the use of postural echo or body language mirroring, plus the constant employment of tie-signs. This made her seem both regal and special *and* accessible, which is a potent blend. Her posture was always impeccable but she flexed her body language communication style to crate empathy with anyone she spoke to. Plus she would dip her head but raise her eyes and use a small suppressed smile. This made her audience feel like a friend she was sharing a joke with.

Tom Cruise

Tom creates his own aura of red-carpet charisma via several very careful techniques. Firstly there is the intriguing blend of specialness combined with accessibility. He has all the trappings of high status and A-list celebrity, always dressing smartly with a dazzling smile and usually a much taller, younger and very beautiful female partner at his side who he appears to choreograph using a series of well-timed body pats. But then he spends exaggeratedly long periods of time meeting and greeting the crowd, posing for mobile snaps and even speaking to relatives on the other end of the phone. Tony Blair tried to ape this technique, using the phone snaps and phone chats trick in an attempt to create a similar sense of celebrity charisma.

Jackie Kennedy

Like Greta Garbo before her, Jackie created a very potent version of enigmatic charisma. She was a political wife in the days when submissive signals were de rigueur and her ability to remain effectively a silent movie star for the rest of her life meant people could adore her without fear of being let down by any verbal messaging. When a character combines beauty and class with a remote silence they allow the audience to project any amount of saint-like or magical qualities on to them.

David Beckham

David is a very obvious example of sporting charisma. In many ways this type of charisma goes with the territory – as kids at school we were all impressed with the specialness of anyone who could achieve greatness in the sporting arena. Being a world-class sportsman or woman only magnifies that effect. David's body language also manages to do what it says on the packet; with his raised chin, one-eyebrow frown, eye fixed on the horizon and undeniable good looks he epitomises the type of manly hero you'd see in any kids' comics.

Business charisma might seem like a lot of hard work, particularly when you're busy or under pressure in your job. However what you've read in this chapter really only amounts to a few simple but effective body language and image tricks that will more than pay back the brief and often one-off effort. Never underestimate the power of your visual impact – get it right and you could find you're doing less work for more money!

Key Points:

- Discover your body language 'type' and flex your style to ensure you communicate effectively with the widest possible group.
- Display charisma and charm where possible.
- Be a good performer.
- Start your performance before you reach the office.
- Effect, don't be affected.
- Give good entrances.
- Give good shake.

13

KILLER OCCASIONS

There are times in every job when you have to stand up and be counted. These are the killer moments, when you're either judged to be a winner or someone who's found wanting.

Networking

Charismatic people are always classy networkers. If the thought of working a room, walking the job or pressing the flesh fills you with terror then don't worry – you're in good company. The first thing to do to resolve any moments of diffidence or irrational dread is to give yourself a little talking to. Business is not some sort of corporate dating agency. To make an impact you must learn how to project yourself with pride and confidence. This means being able to walk up to people (often total strangers) introduce yourself and do small talk.

Working a room

- When you're in what is cheesily referred to as a 'networking opportunity' (which is arguably most of your life), never hunt in packs or pairs. Working alone means no chance to stand chatting to someone you know well already.

- Set targets. Eight intros and chats per hour is good, it will keep the momentum going.

- Get a drink but don't pause after that or you'll stall. If you start getting too picky you'll put off working the room.

- Avoid groups of two or solo people. Go for threesomes if you can as they'll be easier to penetrate.

- See the gap in the group you're going to stand in and walk towards it with energy. When a group sees a fast-moving object bearing down on it it will widen that gap. Lurk too creepily and they're likely to close it to keep you out.

- If you find yourself hovering because they won't let you in, wait only two seconds then wave to a pretend person across the room and walk off.

- When you're in the gap introduce yourself silently by looking and smiling at the people on either side.

- Never interrupt the speaker as they have the alpha role, albeit temporarily.

- While they're speaking gain acceptance from the group by using mirroring techniques. Copy their pace, energy and type of body language.

- When the alpha finishes making his or her point slide in under the radar by complimenting or agreeing with it, or even ask a question about the subject matter. Then when you have everyone's attention introduce yourself, using eye contact and a genuine smile.

- Remember groups aren't always polite or accepting. Especially groups of people who hate networking and suffer from their own insecurities. They might be so smug they've been accepted that they want to see you suffer as they've done in the past. You might be treated like the runt of the litter but that doesn't mean you have to think like one or act like one.

- Be careful where you hold your glass: waist height will project openness and confidence. Higher and it starts to look like a barrier.

- Be careful what you eat. In fact only eat if you're hosting and your guest is eating. Eat to keep them company, not because you're hungry. It's almost impossible to eat party food and look charismatic at the same time. I don't think I've ever seen a charismatic person eating when working a room. If you must eat, avoid danger foods like pastry, chicken legs, sandwiches with tomato or funny lettuce in them, salad (unless it's finely chopped) and anything runny. Don't forget the difficulties of holding a glass and a plate. Your call! I suggest you eat before you go.

- Never queue for the buffet.

- Never fill your plate or pile it high.

- Never take food or drink home with you.

- Don't be too quick with the business cards. In the UK it looks cheesy and desperate.

- Mirror the person you're talking to. Slightly and subtly copy their pose and energy. Aim for something unisex. I watched a man networking with a group of women at an event and he stood with his legs splayed, rocking on his heels and fiddling with change in his pocket. The effect was more like some god-awful mating ritual than an attempt at business networking.

- I once watched Bill Clinton do the shoulder-grab to great effect. He was talking to Putin and wanted to bring in Blair. So he placed a firm but friendly hand on Putin's shoulder and steered him across to Blair, then kept his hand on Putin's shoulder throughout the introductions and opening conversation. It was high-status, yes, and I'd baulk about recommending you try it. But it was such a brave, sturdy and in-control piece of networking that I was breathless with admiration. He'd taken Putin across but not dumped him when he got there.

- Use eye contact and active listening signals like nodding, pacing and mirroring. Never look round the room while the other person is speaking and never look at your watch.

- When you want to get away start to open your body out towards the room and discuss networking with your group, as in, 'Who should we be introduced to?' If you're hosting the event make sure you take your guest across to meet another guest, never dump them. Do introductions and introduce a topic of mutual interest.

Business Presentations

These are the Academy Award-winners of the business world in terms of performance moments. Although relatively new on the corporate landscape they've gained sufficient speed, power and energy to become everyone's favourite way of creating embarrassment, pain and tedium. A presentation can be brief and informal, performed to an audience as small as one, or large rambling beasties that hold huge cavernous auditoriums of City types in their thrall – or not, as the case may be.

Three key facts to remember about business presentations:

1 No one likes giving them.
2 Everyone hates listening to them.
3 Even if you haven't done one yet the chances are you will have to do one at some stage, so you'd better make the

most of it and gird your loins and learn some tips while you can.

Why put yourself through this mutual pain-barrier? Are business presentations merely a form of sado-masochism? Would you be better off beating yourself with birch twigs in front of an invited audience?

The key thing to keep in mind about presentations is that they can inspire, motivate, entertain and drive people like no other form of communication. Leaders use speeches to mesmerise millions of people at a time. Show me a really good speaker and I'll show you someone who can change people's minds for good or for evil.

My bitch is with the speakers who range from 'quite good' to mediocre to dull. Especially the ones who want to get up there behind the lectern because they're usually the only ones who like the sound of their own voice. So don't worry if you have a dread of making business presentations. It's the people who *don't* who probably shouldn't be up there in the first place. They're a bit like a teenager easing themselves into the driving seat of a Ferrari – no matter how keen and how confident they might feel they just haven't realised the dangers involved in making a mistake. The very worst presenters are the ones who think they're doing something wonderful. This means they're often long-winded and extremely smug.

Presenters often feel their audience is their enemy but this is not true. You and your audience will share one vital view in common and that is that neither of you want to be there. Understanding this basic fact will enable you to make the most of your presentations.

Twenty golden rules of business presentations

1 *Never try to take the body language factor away*

Just because you're bricking it doesn't mean you should attempt to remove yourself from the presentation process. By this I mean putting the whole thing on to slides and then standing with your back turned to the audience, reading out loud. I call this 'Business Karaoke'. You are the presentation, not your slides. Repeat after me: PowerPoint is boring.

2 *Wear comfy shoes*

No, I'm not talking slippers or old trainers but I do mean shoes that give your body a good strong grounding. Shoes you can move in, too. I've had some of my most hideous presenting experiences in shoes that looked good but that became a liability.

3 *Warm up in the toilet*

Shake your hands in the air to relax them, breathe out deeply, hum to get your voice moving, bounce about to warm your body up and please do adjust your clothing and all before you are visible. Never walk up to the stage hiking up your trousers or checking your flies. No actor would ever go out on stage still getting into their costume.

4 *Empty your pockets*

If you have anything in your trouser pockets you'll start fiddling with it. Take off any other fiddle-objects, like rings or necklaces, too.

5 *Take a moment*

Never start talking before you're into position. Some people are yapping as they walk up to their spot. When you reach the place where you've planned to speak from get into your pole position and pause. Look around at your audience. Smile. Focus. Then speak. Remember the firing range dictum: Ready...Take Aim...Fire! This is your steady and take aim stage.

6 *Stand, don't sit*

Why? Surely if you stand you give everyone a chance to see your quivering legs and shaking hands? No, that's a joke. Standing has power and energy. Sitting is too easy-going on your audience. Would you sit to tell people to evacuate a room in the case of a fire? Then you should never sit when you want to add impact to your message.

7 *Walk away from the lectern*

Who invented those things? Horrible, horrible, horrible.

8 *Watch the props*

Keep your hands empty. Anything you clutch in them will be something you cling to for comfort. Never carry notes or cue-cards. Put them somewhere nearby but never hold them in your hand. No pens, no pointers, no nothing.

9 *Get into pole position*

That is, your Power Pose, as described earlier in this book (page 61).

10 *Start with a laugh*

Not a huge belly-laugh but just a small joke as an ice-breaker. The important ice it should be breaking is your own. When you laugh at your own humour your smile will make your face muscles relax, you'll let out all that air you've been holding in your lungs and your shoulder muscles will become less tense. Endorphins will be released in your body making you happy and all will be well in the world.

11 *Use eye contact but don't abuse it*

It's good to look in the direction of your audience but

never imagine you need to pin them with your steely stare for longer than it takes to blink. In fact you probably don't need to look them in the eye at all as too much staring can embarrass them. When you're searching for words it will feel useful to stare up and ahead as that eye position is good for accessing memorised words. However it will create a cut-off from your audience, as will turning round to look at your screen.

12 *Use a friendly face*

Smile. Imagine you're greeting a room full of friends. Never look nervous or defensive. There is a widely held belief that visual signals of nervousness or submission will elicit a response from your audience of pity or empathy. Believe me, it won't. The minute a speaker lets his or her audience know they're nervous the audience start to hate them for wasting their time. Nobody loves an amateur these days.

13 *Use your hands when you speak*

But use them for the power of good, not evil. Your hand gestures should add emphasis, not heckle or distract. Use open gestures that are illustrative or that supply emotional back-up.

14 *Keep your hands low*

When your hands creep up to shoulder height you're beginning to signal nervousness or panic. By the time they've gone above your shoulders you're not waving, you're drowning. Keep your gestures around waist- to chest-height.

15 *Move*

Nobody said you should stand still when you present, least of all me. Walk and talk at the same time because it will add energy to your message. Beware the three stage-walkers' no-no's, though:

- Pacing like a lion at feeding time. It makes you look psychotic.
- Doing a dance that The Shadows perfected in the early 60s. Okay, so you're too young to remember but it was something along the lines of two steps forward, cross your legs, two steps back...
- Standing in front of your LitePro. You should never be wearing your slides across your chest. And when that strong light burns into your eyes the rabbit-caught-in-headlights stare that ensues is not a good look.

16 *Walk forward when you've been asked a question*

Even if it's the killer question, the one that's just dragged itself up from the bowels of hell to stop you in your tracks, you should always look as though you're pleased someone asked it. Use eye contact on the questioner, take a couple of steps towards him or her, repeat the question with a tone of delight and never fold your arms or back away. That way everyone in the audience will be fooled into thinking you know the answer, even if you fluff your verbal response.

17 *Avoid body barriers*

Arm-folding, face-touching and self-hugging should all be avoided. The self-hug is a gesture that can be performed with your arms at your sides. It's when you press your arms against your sides in an apparent bid to squeeze your torso like a tube of toothpaste. When you're listening to a member of your audience speak, though, you could place one arm across your chest in a demi-arm-fold, with the other elbow propped on to the hand. This implies concentrated listening.

18 *Pit-bare*

Not aggressively (that is, hands behind head) but just make sure you allow a little air to come up under your armpits. Relax your shoulders and drop them, then move your arms away from your sides slightly.

19 *Avoid an unfinished symphony*

One of the most annoying and distracting gestures you can use while presenting is the half-baked or unfinished one. An example is the aborted countdown, when a speaker says, 'There are five key points here,' holds his or her fingers up in the air, counts off one or two then forgets to make the other points but continues to hold the fingers aloft. Or the speaker who starts to take the lid off the flipchart pen then stops and waves it around instead.

20 *Know how to close*

Your end pose should be one of the key moments of your talk. This is often the lowest point for speakers though because they begin that peculiar ritual known as the 'denial dance'. If you've spoken well and made some good points now's the time to close with confidence and a small bow to acknowledge the applause. Instead, though, a majority of speakers choose this moment to throw scorn on everything they've just said. The denial dance is usually either the pulling of a small face, including an eye-roll, or a dismissive hand-flap or a shrug of the shoulders or even a quasi-funny crab-walk back to your seat. All this is a last-ditch attempt to seek liking and sympathy, often in the fear that what you've just said might have been controversial or just a bit assertive. It's your subconscious trying to apologise for all your well-made points by pulling a comic pose but all I can say is that if you're thinking of doing it, *don't*!

How to Sell

Selling is a funny old business. As soon as a new technique hits the streets everyone jumps on to the bandwagon and it becomes stale and hackneyed before you can say 'patter'.

All the tricks of the trade seem to have had their day now although some sales people cling on to them like Linus clung on to his comfort blanket. The problem is one of saturation. Everyone's at it. I went to collect a prescription from the chemist last week and the poor woman had to ask me if I'd also like to buy stamps or a mobile phone top-up. Banks try add-on selling to the point where they've devalued the function of a bank, and even chuggers in the street who try to get you signed up for charity donations have made the pavements a new point-of-sale.

With this in mind it's probably better to work to two rules:

1 Don't be coy about the fact that you're selling something. I think there's very little that's worse than the 'I wouldn't be doing my job if I didn't recommend you open this new account' line they take in building societies or the 'Can you spare time for a survey?' approach that masks a hard sell. If you're shirty about selling whatever it is then they should rightly be shirty about buying. How bad can a product or service be that even the salesperson doesn't want to admit they're selling it?

2 Create rapport. And if you think you create rapport by overuse of a person's first name or a 'best friend' tone to your voice you're wrong. The process of sales rapport is not the same as making a new best friend.

I've described the skills of body language rapport in other chapters and the rules don't change when you're selling. Remember the values you're trying to promote:

- Enthusiasm
- Honesty
- Knowledge
- Marginally lower status

So, here's a list of things to keep in mind when you're selling:

- Never treat your customer as someone to score points off. Lay off the power shake and the alpha body language signals.
- Use eye contact to show honesty but don't overdo it
- Mirror their body language in terms of pace and posture – but do it subtly!
- Pace yourself – it's good to look calm. Avoid nervous body language rituals or self-comfort rituals. Drop your shoulders and breathe out.
- Avoid overcongruence. It is the enemy of honesty.
- Drop a few points to win a few. If you admit to small losses or negatives now and again people will be prepared to believe your positives.

Making Your Presence Felt at Business Meetings

- Always be punctual.
- Never walk in carrying a cup of tea or a sandwich.
- Only carry papers.
- Sit in a seat that is diagonal to the most powerful person.
- Sit facing the door.

- Never sit squashed against a wall – space means power.
- Don't hang your jacket over the back of your chair.
- If you're in charge sit at the top of the table or create a 'Last Supper' formation (see page 260).
- Always pick a chair with armrests.
- Sit into the back of the chair but never slump.
- Don't help yourself to tea and biscuits.
- The only prop you have should be a pen but don't abuse your pen! See tips on pages 283–4.
- Shake hands, offering yours first if you're hosting the meeting.
- Don't give out business cards until the end of the meeting.
- Make a written note of names and who's sitting where but don't let others see you doing it.
- Always say something within the first three minutes.
- Use rotational eye contact, picking out everyone around the table.
- Be an active listener, nodding when people talk.
- Never become inactive; like a jogger stopping to cross a street, it's hard to get the momentum going to get back up to speed again.
- Never create body barriers with folded arms or your hands over your body.
- Be prepared to stand if necessary to make your killer points, but only if you need the floor for a long period of time.
- If you do stand make sure you're fully upright before you start speaking. Take a moment.
- Use announcement gestures to let people know you're about to speak, like a lightly raised arm, sitting forward and placing your hands on the table, taking off your glasses, raising both hands, palms frontward, etc.

- Never speak from your listening position; it lacks drama and effect. Always change your state before you speak.
- Be a good, attentive listener because it means you should deserve the same back. If you interrupt people, talk over them or ignore them you're creating bad karma.
- Use your hand gestures to add value and emphasis to your points.
- If you want the attention of an individual you can get it and keep it by raising a finger or a pen up to eye level and looking at them.
- Keep your points short and concise and your body language dynamic.
- One of the least popular body language routines during meetings will come from the serial moaner. He or she will make their point with barely disguised irritation or suppressed anger or frustration. They sit back in their seat with their arms folded and they always execute what I call the 'turkey neck-wobble' as they speak. Their favourite phrases are: 'That's all very well, but...' or simply 'Yes, but...' Don't become them. Keep open body language gestures, a positive facial expression and good eye contact.

Business meetings can be a foul abuse of your time but rather than dying of boredom take steps to get the most out of them. Never use them as an opportunity to sit in silence over a cuppa. Instead see them as a platform for your own ideas as well as sharing and swapping thoughts with others. This requires energy and input, and remember that when you do speak you also need to take steps to make sure the other attendees listen.

Pen abuse

Your pen will be your constant companion at work and – without you realising it – will also become a barometer of your inner thoughts and feelings. Make sure your penwork isn't giving away more than you wanted.

- **The sword**

  You brandish it aloft when you're on the attack, jabbing it like a sword or stabbing it like a dagger. It displays a suppressed desire to launch a physical attack.

- **The metronome**

  You tap it on your desk or on your hand, either all the time or sometimes as you make your big point. It looks aggressive and controlling.

- **The scientist**

  You take it to pieces and put it back together again, unscrewing the middle and then stuffing everything back once the spring makes it all fall out. It makes you look nervous and clumsy or hugely distracted.

- **The chewer**

  You chew the top of your pen like a chipmunk chews a log. When you've finished a large part of the plastic is missing and the end looks gnarled, with teeth puncture-marks. You look anxious and frustrated, with a high degree of suppressed aggression.

- **The sucker**

  You suck the top of your pen. This is a very childlike comfort gesture, like sucking your thumb. It can also have sexual overtones if you pull it slowly in and out of your mouth.

- **The clicker**

  You make your pen click at regular intervals with the pace increasing as the pressure builds up. You look stressed and anxious and you annoy the hell out of your colleagues.

- **The helicopter**

  You spin your pen around between your fingers like a rotating helicopter blade. You look childish and bored.

- **The doodler**

  Your doodling is probably done to increase your listening power but it will look as though you're bored.

Front-Line Bodytalk

Despite the tidal wave of customer care training and theorising, people who deal with the public for a living are usually dire when it comes to simple transactional skills. The worst are the ones who believe they're 'people' people. They usually manage to patronise or act like an overeager extra from the set of *Blue Peter*. Some are exceptionally rude. At times I feel like doffing my hat and bowing to their advances in techniques in making the punter feel small.

Front-line work is really a doddle though. The public are secretly easily pleased. It's just that when those small shreds of status that we like to hold so dear get put through yet another pulping machine we tend to fight back or turn on our heel and go off for good.

My advice for front-line body language is going to be terribly, terribly basic. You'll say you know it all already but – as I always tell the delegates on my training courses – there's a whole wide world between *knowing* and *doing*. Simple though these steps are, they're also absolutely vital, and front-line staff who get them all right are as rare as hen's teeth.

- Acknowledge people straight away. Not once they've got to your desk or counter, and definitely not once you've finished what you're doing. Good front-line staff have huge antennae stalking out of their foreheads. They twitch when a customer is even in the vicinity. They know when someone is about to walk in and they're looking up the moment they do. If you're busy on a call or with another customer just catch their eye and nod. They'll probably weep with gratitude.

- Give polite 'wait' signals. One raised finger that is slightly bent will do, or a small smile and nod. Maybe even a few fingers held up to show you'll only be a couple of minutes.

- Smile. And make it a good one. Look genuinely pleased to see the customer. Not over-eager or relieved, and don't smile as though they're the very best thing that's ever happened in your life. But do execute a nice smile that looks friendly. Make sure it's in your eyes, too.

- Ignore their lack of response. If you're smiling in the hope that everyone will smile back and the world will suddenly be made of candy and bluebirds will start whistling songs from *Mary Poppins*, you're delusional. Whatever your face does and no matter how good your smile is, it's likely you'll be looking at a deadpan or even scowling response. The good news is that it doesn't matter one whit! Whatever our faces do – and I'm speaking for customers everywhere here – we're thinking our smile inside. It's just that it could take a few years before it reaches our lips. We've often been commuting and that means we've spent an hour or two dogfacing.

- Lean forward slightly when you first speak. It shows an intention and a desire to help.

- Use eye contact.
- Tilt your head very slightly to one side. Not too much or you'll look sickeningly cute.
- Keep appropriate space between you and your customer. Around four feet is good, unless you're being pushy for a sale in which case make it a little more.
- Keep in mind the status balance. Buyers are always considered higher in status than sellers. It doesn't mean you have to grovel but your body language should reflect that fact. Receptionists who look pompous or up themselves will annoy the hell out of a customer. Look confident and in control but never stand more upright or look more relaxed than your customer. Avoid basic status displays too, like hands on hips, too much eye contact or a puffed chest.
- Illustrate your instructions with your gestures. If you're working on a hotel desk or reception you'll already be aware that punters take stupid pills before they walk into the building. We can't take directions and we're terribly bad at listening to instructions. Tell us our room is on the left and we'll go to the right. Say 'second floor' and we'll take the lift to the fourth. And you don't even want to see us struggling with the lighting and the electric kettle or the shower once we get into the room. Never patronise but remember that by miming how to place that plastic card in the door lock or how we should turn right once we get out of the lift we're much less likely to come back and ask for more help.
- Stand, don't sit. I hate reception desks with a very deep loathing. They're outmoded, outdated and they need to be re-invented. When you go to a posh hotel or a large, ritzy company you have to queue at them in exactly the

same way that you have to queue at the post office. One major UK company has just introduced the idea of hosting a lobby rather than having the reception desk set-up and I'm breathless in admiration. Walking to approach a visitor is miles better than making them queue at a desk.

- Keep your computer in its place. Never let it get above its station. It's the customer that counts, not some uppity screen and keyboard combo. Never have your eyes fixed to your screen when your customer is about.

- Never over-lower your status. Customers like to be dealt with by someone who looks confident, knowledgeable and in control of their area. Looking nervous or grovelling won't work.

- If you deal with a complaint or an irate client use a technique called matching and pacing to influence them to calm down. Telling someone to be calm will only make their anger turn into rage. Instead, make sure your body language mirrors some of their distress to enable you to reach some stage of empathy. This means you apply an expression of concern to your face via a slight raising of the eyebrows, a subtle lean forward and a posture that says you're ready to help sort their problem out. If their pace of movement is fast then yours should speed up a little. If they're using dramatic gestures then yours should be a little bit bigger. Listen to their problem then start to bring them down by defusing their anger rather than intensifying it. Mirror – pace – lead. Slightly copy, then become slowly calmer yourself and they should take your lead and become less irate.

- When you're using mirroring to create rapport or empathy always take your lead from the customer. If they look cheery or chatty, follow suit. If they're quieter or more formal, formalise your own body language. Never go for the push. Pushing is when you try to change their state regardless of their own feelings. Has this ever happened to you? You're walking along the high street and a charity mugger approaches being cheeky and persistent. You push your way past them and into your bank. Inside they've strung up balloons and a perky greeter asks in a sing-song voice what they can do for you today. This type of approach is called scorched earth and it takes no heed of the customer's mood or feelings.

- Having said that, I do feel it's vital, even in brief transactions, for you to 'make the customer's day'. Connect but don't overdo it. Smile, display friendly body language and have a very brief friendly word with them. Be sympathetic if it's raining or crack a small joke if they're looking cheerful. Often it's the very smallest transactions that make someone's day worthwhile.

How to Get a Pay Rise

Remember, when these amazing tips work I want a cut of the profits!

- Plan your approach. Never work on instinct. Leaping into the lift with your boss and calling that an opportunity to chat about your job is reckless to the point of being extremely dumb.
- Do masses of pre-meet work. In the weeks or months leading up to your 'ask' you should be raising your profile and exhibiting all those reasons why your boss should be awarding you more dosh.

- Be punctual and be seen looking keen and vigorous. Sit near the front at meetings and make positive points. Visualise what a vital employee of your company would look like and then become that person. Go for visuals above proper work. There's absolutely no point working late or turning up early if the boss isn't there to see you.

- Target the big cheese. It is completely pointless to spend one whisker of time trying to look good to anyone other than the person who will be making the decision about your pay rise. It is a good rule in business to trust no one. Therefore jumping through body language and image hoops in the hope your line manager will report favourably on you to the HR manager or whoever is probably going to be time wasted. Always perform in front of your target audience; never work by proxy.

- Make an appointment for your 'ask'. Choose the time carefully. Are they a morning or afternoon person? When does their job get really busy? When do they prefer to mellow and chat? What time do they like to leave work? Tune in to their thinking and mood patterns.

- Try not to drop hints. People are easier to persuade if they're caught on the hop, before they've had time to formulate their response. If you're asked for a reason for the meeting, try the Trojan Horse technique, telling them it's about the order numbers in accounts then adding the pay rise on to the agenda once you're in the meeting.

- Look as though you expect a favourable response. It's hard to say no to people who are looking keen, open and friendly. If you look defensive or aggressive you'll have done half their work for them already, making it much easier for them to say what you're obviously already thinking.

- Face them front on, sit upright and don't fiddle. Use eye contact as you ask for the pay rise and never drop your gaze at the crucial point. Avoid face-touch or face-covering gestures or you'll look defensive or as if you don't believe your own points.

- Keep it simple. Simple points to persuade and simple body language to back them up and make them look convincing.

- When you tell them why you should have a pay rise, make your reasons sound as if they're for their benefit rather than your own. Although it might be valid to say you're up to your ears in mortgage, it will have a greater influential effect if you can tell them why the business will gain from your added income. This is called the WIIFM principle: 'What's in it for me?'

- Never use signals of suppressed aggression or challenge. It only makes it easier for them to say no. Workplace conflicts never lead to resolution. Never offer threats or you'll kick off a status or power battle that only a boss can win.

- For this reason keep your own body language slightly subservient to theirs, although always display confidence. If you look overpowering you might even make them *want* to say no. There have been many moments when I have been keen to make changes to suit the person talking to me but their attitude has made me relish the opportunity to turn them down.

- Never display signs of suppressed anything. Sitting in front of your boss looking like a volcano about to erupt will only ever change their state for the worse. Breathe out and leave all emotional baggage outside the room. Red faces, hands balled into fists, bulging eyes, tearful eyes, lip-chewing, hand-wringing or baleful staring will do nothing to add value to your argument. Look intelligent and reasonable.

- Emotion is better issued verbally in the workplace. Physical displays tend to be the equivalent of losing face, which is why a proper leader is usually portrayed as calm at all times. Nobody's stopping you from discussing your feelings, though. Keep in mind that a non-verbal display of anger or upset will normally turn people off and devalue your point but saying something like 'I have to tell you that I feel very angry about this' and dishing it up with calm logical body language and vocal tone will make your message far more potent.

How to Have an Office Romance

All affairs begin, occur and end in a welter of body language signals that are always far too potent and obvious to mask with any ease. There's something intrinsically funny about sex at work. Maybe it's the cultural clash, with offices that are primarily set up for logical, planned thinking and behaviour suddenly suffering a tidal wave of unbridled emotions, or perhaps it's the way that employees who are normally responsible adults can turn into reckless teens keen to throw all caution to the winds as they start groping or even having sex at office parties or photographing their bare behinds on the office photocopier.

It affects the highest in the land. Who can forget that shot of John Prescott holding his PA aloft looking less like a deputy PM and more like an alpha ape? Or the mental image created by stories of Monica Lewinsky and the cigar?

There's obviously a serious side to all this as well, but for anyone thinking of embarking on some workplace sexual shenanigans and expecting to be able to keep it all under wraps, here's your thought for the day: *you won't*!

Why not? Well your body language will give you away. Office or workplace environments tend to create a lot of in-tune people. There's a colony feel to the teams and groups that form and, like any animal colony, survival depends on the ability to read and sense one another's non-verbal messages. Sexual non-verbal messages don't take a lot of sensing. For a start there's a natural desire to pair people off. Every colony has its own speed-dating section and if two of its members tend to register as a possible match their names will have come up in people's minds and they'll get monitored. So some simple points if you're trying to bury your affair:

- **Never ignore one another**

  Ignoring is the oldest trick in the book and the most easily sussed. Once you're into your affair or even just embarking on it you'll have an instinctive desire to over-react when the object of your affection's name is mentioned. To suppress and mask this urge to blush, giggle or suddenly pay massive attention you'll probably over-perform in the other direction and start ignoring them instead. Far from throwing people off the scent it will only increase speculation, especially if you're ignoring someone who sits at the next desk.

- **Do arrive together**

  Arriving apart is the surest sign of guilt, especially if you're caught dropping your sex-mate off around the corner from the premises and making them walk the last bit. There's something about sod's law, too, that says the more effort you put into arriving separately the more events will conspire to make you pitch up at the same time. I know one couple who would split up about a mile from the premises and he'd finish the journey on a collapsible bike. By the time she'd parked and he'd collapsed his bike again, they inevitably ended up colliding in the revolving doors at the front of the building.

- **Don't stare**

  Staring is an inevitable by-product of falling in love and lust but you'll need to tone it down if you don't want to scream your affair from the rooftops. If you can't help yourself there's only one way out: use exactly the same amount of eye contact on all your other colleagues.

- **Do flirt**

  But just a bit. Flirting is quite natural in most companies, albeit in a non-sexual way, so suddenly stopping will look suspicious.

- **Don't suddenly start flirting with other people**

  This doesn't throw co-workers off the scent; it just makes them swivel their gun-sights on to your partner to see how he or she is reacting. Laughing maniacally while the person you love is draped over a colleague is a hard stunt to pull off.

SPECIALITIES OF THE HOUSE

Some body language tips are rather more specialised and possibly even risky. However that shouldn't mean you can't have access to them. I'm no great fan of politicians when it comes to image and non-verbal signals but I still find it fascinating to study all their little tricks of the trade. Although I'm not advocating you use them, there are still points to be learnt and possibly some techniques you'd like to put into your own repertoire.

How to Be Prime Minister

There's a lot to be learnt from studying the image profile of a country's president or prime minister. On the one hand it tells us a lot of information about the head of state, but on the other it is hugely revealing in terms of the people who vote for them. It's been many years since people voted purely for policies. The further back in time you go the more disconnected the leader. These days we are all far more confident and self-assured and think that the role of leadership – like celebrity – is achievable and accessible. We don't look for specialness any more, we look for similarities to ourselves. Where Harold Wilson was a patriarchal figure and Thatcher was our headmistress, Tony Blair was the bloke next door who you'd see shovelling the kids into the back of the people-carrier every morning on the school run. George W. Bush has the attitude of a friendly guy you'd meet in a bar.

Accessible or not, though, all modern leaders have to be image-aware. Awareness doesn't always mean success, but even the failures give us clues for behaviour that we can take into our working lives, especially if you're going for a top job.

- **Height**
  This is really an issue of stature, rather than inches. Most current leaders are tall, although not over-tall. Those that aren't, like Putin or Hillary Clinton, will accentuate their stature by standing tall. In the case of Condoleezza Rice, Hillary Clinton and Margaret Thatcher they accentuate their height by wearing big hair. When Thatcher took us

to war, her hairstyle became bigger and more rigid. Like a helmet.

- **Hair**

Which brings us on to the subject of hair. It is common knowledge that hair is a vote-winner. Why? I think it might have something to do with instant identification. Your hair colour, length and style create an instant image in people's minds. There has always been a link (erroneous, of course) between hair and virility. For many people baldness is linked with both old age and babyhood. All I hear about Prince William now is that he's 'losing his hair'. This matters less for a modern leader, though, since head-shaving has become an acceptable solution.

- **Facial expressions**

All political leaders know the importance of honing a couple of signature expressions. Blair loved his raised-brow-and-smile bloke-ish face and his mouth-shrug, raised-eye, fast-blink look of regret in the face of tragedy. However, George W. Bush is more of a one-trick pony. If the twinkle-eyed, suppressed-but-shared-smile look isn't appropriate he'll use it anyway. Harold Wilson employed a pipe as his prop to do his expression for him and Thatcher honed a rather regal look, with her eyes raised and slightly narrowed and a high-status, closed-lip smile.

- **Walk**

Intentional walking is important. Thatcher would always walk quickly to suggest decisiveness and energy. During the war Bush and Blair both discovered the Power Walk, 100 per cent testosterone-fuelled, which was presumably supposed to impress the public and terrify the enemy, almost as though the two men were intending to get stuck into the fighting themselves. They took large strides and held their arms away from their sides, signalling the kind of muscle-bound look you get with wrestlers and night-club bouncers.

Both Hillary Clinton and Condoleezza Rice have developed something of a military stride that they use during very important meetings. Bill Clinton had a less remarkable walk but his height and stature would always create a diversion and so would his constant use of the wave.

- **Leakage**

All politicians have a whole raft of leakage gestures but the good ones learn to contain them. Some still have a habit of believing they're off-camera right up until they start to speak, which is something the royals and certain celebrities have learnt isn't true. One of Blair's greatest leakage gestures would come from his thumbs. He had a habit of doing the gated hands gesture, with hands held out in front of his torso, palms towards his body and fingers held together. When he was on top of his game the thumbs would be erect, like a cocked gun. When he was less assured they'd be slightly bent.

Gestures

Political leaders (and some royals) employ several critical power techniques to reinforce their status when they're out and about. One of the most important is the gesticulation pecking order.

- **Powerful hands**

It's vital for the top guy to be seen to be the one doing all the gesticulating when they're walking and talking with other people. By being the gesticulator it looks as though they're the one in charge and the one asking keen questions and gathering information. It's interesting that women, especially royal women, are often given bunches of flowers to carry to prevent them doing this powerful gesture. It's almost as though we're still not happy with a woman being visually in charge and even female leaders have to look compliant.

- **Me me me**

  Although leaders will be happy to use the empty embrace gesture to keep the audience engaged and connected it's easy to see what the core message is when the chips are down. When you want to big yourself up to your boss I bet you still struggle with the word 'I', as in 'I got that big contract'. For modesty purposes we prefer to say 'we' and hope the boss gets the real message. Politicians know exactly how to get that real message across, though. When they want to imply personal endeavour or ownership they use 'me me me' gestures. Blair's gated hands would rise higher and tend to close up, creating an isolated look as though he was peering over the walls of a small castle. This created an aura of separateness and high authority. The chest-poke is another common ruse. By turning their fingers inward and poking them at around heart level they signal the word 'me' very strongly.

- **The circuit-breaker**

  All leaders have to mask their true feelings a lot of (if not most of) the time. This masking can cause massive inner distress and almost unbearable effort, which is why they use the circuit-breaker to create a vital pause and rest. Usually the trick is to take a sip of water. This allows them to drop their face along with the mask they're wearing for a vital few seconds and it usually implies they're aware they're suffering from mask-slippage. The break allows them to refresh the mask, like a woman refreshing her make-up. Tony Blair did a vital refresh when he was getting booed by the Women's Institute, and Clinton employed both a can of drink and a glass of water when he was interviewed about Monica Lewinsky.

- **The thumb of power**

  There are some hand gestures that tend to exist primarily in the political arena and the thumb of power is one of them. There's no reason why you shouldn't copy it though if the moment seems right. Politicians were once told not to point, so the rigid digit was rarely used, even in heated debates. Instead the knuckle-point became popular, with the fingers bent into the palm and the index finger knuckle used as a pointer to add emphasis to the words. As an added power gesture the thumb would then be placed over the top knuckle, emphasising dominance.

- **Measuring hands**

  Another political staple are the measuring hands. Both hands are held out with elbows bent at right angles and the hands are quite rigid and placed palm-facing-palm with a gap between them. The size of the gap is used to signal the size of the problem that the government or individual faces. Once the problem has been explained the gesture will nearly always be followed up by a precision gesture to show it's all under control.

- **Precision gesture**

  This is a superb gesture that can be used for both attack and defence. Under attack it will imply the speaker knows exactly what to do and how to deal with a problem and when used for an attack it implies a very definite and superior strategy. The hand is held out and the fingertips pinched together, with the hand being rocked slightly as you speak.

- **The chop**

  Another political favourite, the chopping hand is a one-hand gesture and implies aggressive decisiveness. If it's just a swipe it can imply reasonable levels of decision-taking or enforcement but if the hand is rigid and the chopping done firmly it says the problem's dealt with and the speaker wants to hear no more about it.

- **The finger- or head-baton**

  Finger-jabbing is now a leadership staple but when the hands aren't used a politician will often employ the head-baton instead. This air-butting gives the impression of emphasis and a willingness to fight strongly for the point. It looks like the final blows in a fight, as though they've already won the argument. Neil Kinnock was a big fan of the baton although he took it to extremes, even going so far as to use the whole-body baton, almost jumping in the air to make his points. One key thing to remember about emphatic gestures: over-use tends to de-emphasise. Ditto with vocal emphasis. Tony Blair was a big user of the emphatic vocal tone but at times devalued it by over-use. Sometimes I would imagine him sitting at home with Cherie saying: 'WOULD – YOU – PASS – THE – SUGAR – PLEASE!'

- **The two-handed gesture**

  Most of us gesture with one hand when we speak. Or at least use one more than the other. In their search to be über-credible and hugely emphatic many political leaders will employ the two-handed gestural technique. Blair and Brown are both huge fans, with Brown performing the Matador Stab – i.e. a two-fingered downward stab gesture – on a regular basis, or even the measuring hands airborne, when the hands are held apart but chopped around in the air as though you're delivering small parcels.

- **The upward point**

Michael Howard was a great fan of the single-digit upward point and his legacy remains. One index finger is held aloft close to the face. This is a gesture of authority and warning that has its roots in schooldays.

- **Rejecting the lectern**

This has gone from being a high-impact shocker to being the norm. You allow your other speakers at a conference to work from behind the comparative safety of a lectern, then you come out and stand directly in front of your audience. The message is you're connecting with them and speaking directly from the heart. It could have won Cameron his place as leader of the Conservative party. John Major used a similar technique years ago when he stood up at conference and took his jacket off to look honest and casual. The contrast with Thatcher's formality was outstanding. However the lectern rejection needs to be applied to the whole speech. Starting behind it then coming around is spooky and scary for your audience. Howard tried this during a keynote speech when he came to the front of the stage to do a tear-jerker bit about his roots. It looked about as choreographed as a scene from *Strictly Ballroom*.

- **Spacial use**

  The bigger the status the more space they use. Blair always took full advantage of space when he was PM.

- **The prop that speaks**

  Political leaders have a clear understanding that a picture speaks a thousand words and will employ props to do their speaking for them. Remember John Major's soapbox or that hankie Thatcher used to cover the new BA logo? Wilson used his pipe to look safe and trustworthy and Blair was rarely seen without a mug of tea in his hand for the same reason. One famous mug even had pictures of his kids on it but then he had the cheek to suggest it wasn't a prop. When did you last leave your house via the front door to go off to work with a mug in your hand without realising it was there?

- **Partnership props**

  Of course the biggest prop a leader can have is the right partner standing by their side when the cameras are about. There's a yin and yang thing with partners and the best ones will be wheeled out to complement the leader or make up for any deficiencies. Hence Hillary suddenly posing with Bill standing behind her when she visits a state that's not too Hillary-friendly. Hence the way Sandra Howard was placed firmly in the limelight during election time to add some fragrant spin to a man described as having 'something of the night' about him.

  Even Denis Thatcher had his moment in the sun when Margaret was first voted in as prime minister. In the early days he was far more visible, often taking the higher-status role, standing in the front of shots or even higher than the leader, suggesting someone might have worried the country wasn't ready for a woman in the seat of power.

A trawl though previous prime ministers throws up some amazing historical contrasts in the role of the political wives and partners. Some stood frozen and low-status like rabbits caught in headlights and others, like Clementine Churchill or Margaret Lloyd George, looked fully able to run the country themselves single-handedly. Clement Attlee's wife brought a necessary touch of fragrance to a man whose smile can only be described as predatory and Mary Wilson wore the look of a woman who had been plucked from her kitchen and left hanging out to dry.

Modern political wives and partners tend to have taken on a quasi-sexual role to make their men look more physically attractive. Key in this movement was Cherie Blair, whose like we'll probably never see again. Clinging to her man like an overexcited limpet, her hugs and glances of adoration suggested we should all worship at the altar of Blair, the sexy superhero. Babies have become very much part of the act too, with even the crustiest of bachelors being pressured into producing offspring to emphasise their youth and virility.

Whether your career path leads you towards No. 10 or in the general direction of corporate IT or accounts, if you intend leading a country or running a reception, you should never forget the power of your non-verbal signals. Jobs can be varied and complex but getting the body language right is relatively simple. Fix your goal first then select the attributes that you'll need to achieve it. Square pegs and round holes never go well together, which is why I often wonder why so many people who choose front-line careers seem to have a pathological hatred of other people, but if you do find yourself in a job that isn't quite a perfect fit you can always hone your acting techniques and nobody will ever need to know.

Key Points:

- Put planning into your appearance for meetings to discuss a pay rise or promotion.
- Front-line body language is full of simple but subtle skills – get your status and submission signals right.
- Pick the right seat at business meetings and be prepared to use announcement gestures to get your points across.
- Business presentations and selling are all about charisma and personal impact. Always remember that you are the message and get your signals right.
- Skip that office romance if you're worried anyone might find out – they'll read your signals however well you try to mask your feelings!
- Take cues from world leaders to up your status in the workplace.
- Networking is constant – you're on display at all times. Monitor your signals and get them to market you at all the key occasions.

14

READING OTHER PEOPLE IN THE WORKPLACE

During our working lives we become consummate body language liars. Even if we enjoy our jobs it's highly unlikely that the workplace is where we would like to be each and every moment of each and every day. Some people hate their jobs so much they'd rather be anywhere else. Some just dislike the people they work with or try to appear more efficient and knowledgeable than they really are.

In body language terms, then, business is all about bluff and double-bluff. Which makes reading and analysing non-verbal signals from your colleagues and clients a bit of a complex issue. Keep in mind the point I made at the start of this book: body language is not a precise science. I'd love to give you direct access to other people's thoughts but it really doesn't work like that. The most fruitful work you can do is on your own body language signals to get your ideal messages across as clearly as possible. The second most fruitful thing you can do is to be more aware of the signals of the people you work with. Assess them and use them to read between the lines and gain much better insights into their true thoughts and meanings. But always keep an open mind to other possibilities. Remember what I said about there being no real 'tells' or absolutes. Never learn your body language lessons like you learnt maths at school. Body language is about algebra but it's called cognitive algebra. There is no formula that says arms folded = aggressive. Or scratched nose = lying. I'd be selling you snake oil if I pretended there was.

Two rules then:

- **Look**

  Easy? Not really. From about the age of two you've been told it's rude to stare so you'll need to slowly advance your perceptual skills and learn to start looking again (only without staring).

- **Evaluate**

  Start with your gut reaction – how did you feel about what they said or did? What did they seem to be signalling to you? Gut reactions are really part of a very complex perceptual process and you shouldn't underestimate strong feelings like this.

  Then think of body language clusters – take any one gesture and put it into the context of the whole body language 'sentence', by which I mean all their other gestures or movements. Attach the gesture to their words, too. Were they congruent, incongruent or overcongruent? Did they agree with their words or heckle them?

  Always remember the Othello Error. However well you assess someone's body language signals you could always be wrong about what prompted them. Othello is warned via a whispering campaign that his wife Desdemona is being unfaithful to him. He questions her, studies her anxious response, judges this to be a sign of guilt and kills her. In fact she was innocent and her signals were prompted by shock at being accused. Right symptoms, wrong cause.

By developing your basic skills of perception – and as long as you're not guilty of that form of assumption known as the Othello Error – you could quadruple your ability to understand your colleagues and clients by doing what's called reading between the lines.

To help your evaluations I'm going to give you a list of feelings and symptoms. Like a doctor you need to read through the symptoms to gain clues to the actual problem, but always keeping an open mind as you do.

How to Look for Signs of Lying

Lying is a very difficult process for the human body, making most of us rather bad liars. First comes the true response, which must be suppressed and the lie response created for the performance. This can cause stress, and guilt prompted by the lie will add to this stress.

It's important to note, though, that not everyone gets stressed when they lie because not everyone feels that sense of guilt. A 'good' liar is often someone who lies regularly and/or believes it is right to tell lies. But the following are some ways in which you could catch a liar:

- Their breathing becomes more frequent and more shallow. This can be visible, you could start to see their chest begin to heave; or vocal, you can hear breathlessness in their voice.

- An adrenalin burst can cause lip-licking and dry mouth. Lip-licking can take several forms. The funniest is the tongue-poke, which is when the tongue emerges from the middle of the lips, which can be a signal of rejection or disgust, like a baby rejecting food. Licking the side of the mouth can mean enjoyment, though, or even flirting.

- Exaggerated swallowing. This is caused by tension in the neck muscles causing throat restriction. Like breathing you might either see this occur or hear the frequent pauses as they fight to swallow.

- Excessive fidgeting. We all fidget but we're not always telling lies. Fidgeting can mean the sympathetic nervous system has kicked in though, promoting a desire to fight or flight. Suppressing this desire can lead to twitchy movements.

- Scratching, especially the back of the head. This auto-contact creates a small feeling of relief and comfort.

- Often eye contact drops at the moment of lie. The liar may feel that their eyes give away too much information. This small 'cut-off' signal can show the moment when the pressure becomes too great.

- Too much eye contact that appears performed. Or they might be aware that looking away appears dishonest and try to opt for prolonged bouts of staring.

- A longer pause before the lie. Verbal stutters are common.
- Eyes moving up and to the right. This can mean they're accessing the creative side of their brain.
- Mouth-touching or -covering. This is another cut-off. It can relate to their child state, when they would have covered their entire face or looked away to lie.

- Nose-touching or -covering. This is another signal of possible facial concealment.
- Blushing. Physiological and impossible to prevent, although it could be prompted by embarrassment.
- Sweating. See blushing above.
- Distraction gestures – using hands or props to distract from what they are saying.

- Throat-clearing. More neck tension and a desire to create a 'thinking and planning' pause.
- Sitting very still, stiller than usual. This can be the poker-face ruse, as in 'If I don't move at all I'll give nothing away with my body language.'
- Becoming more expressive, waving hands and being long-winded. This is the body language version of verbal diarrhoea.
- Hand gestures occur after their words. When they speak the truth their gestures should come first as the easiest expression of feelings and thoughts.
- Exaggerated palm displays. Although some palm display can look honest and open, too much might be overcongruent.

- Puffing to release tension.
- Speech disturbances – stammering, repetition, pauses.

How to Look for Signs of Rejection or Being Dismissive

- Brushing hand across knee or thigh as though brushing away crumbs. Those invisible crumbs could be symbolic of your thoughts or ideas.
- Shrugging. This gesture really does mimic a throwing off

of ideas or situations. If they do this in reply to your idea or conversation it's likely they're casting it off, but it could apply to their own speech, so look for the moment of shrug and what's being said at the time.

- Head-shaking. This mimics a child rejecting the breast and is one of the most basic human body language signals.
- Folding arms and leaning back in chair. Again, check timing. These barrier gestures can signal rejection.
- Breathing in and looking upward. Eyes can be used to produce intentional signals – e.g. show a desire to escape or look heavenwards for inspiration or help. This gesture suggests they're digging deep for inspiration or thought. Not a good sign for acceptance!
- Pursing lips or sucking lips in. This implies a retention of negative words, thoughts or feelings.
- Tapping. This metronomic gesture can signal they want the conversation to end.
- Neck-wobble. This is likely to mean aggression is building.
- Hand raised. Often to stop or block speech.
- Turning away when talking. This very basic form of rejection also could be a sign of shyness, though.
- Eye-dart. This can mean mixed feelings, including panic or a desire to escape.
- Sitting back in chair, looking downward. They could be lost in thought but they could also be hiding negative responses.
- Carrying on working. This often prompts cognitive dissonance in the speaker – that is, it's such a big sign of rejection that we almost think they can't really be that rude and continue speaking. But they *can* be that rude.

- Staring at their screen. This is an intentional gesture that can imply they'd rather be dealing with anything more interesting, even their screensaver!
- Fast nodding. A non-verbal interruption.
- Hand-flapping. Could be a sign of enjoyment but more likely to signal drowning.
- Looking at watch!

How to Spot Possible Signs of Stress or Anxiety

- Shoulders tense and raised – the stress symptoms include muscle tension with the most visible being the shoulders.
- Excessive self-calm or self-comfort rituals, like self-hug, self-stroke or facial touch.
- Nail-biting, scratching, lip-biting rituals. Self-attacks can be a sign of suppressed aggression but will mainly hint at stress.
- Fiddling. This is normal but can increase with stress. If you don't know what's normal for this person always search for other symptoms to endorse the diagnosis.
- Tapping. Stressed people can feel the pressure of time at all times. Tapping can be a metronomic gesture showing a constant desire to hurry.
- Looking towards the exit. Eye-gaze can register intentions or desires, in this case a desire to escape.
- Barriers like folded arms or drinks or bags held high to chest. If they look like an auto-contact body-hug they could signal stress or anxiety.
- Excessive straightening gestures: notes, ties, hair, pens, etc. Stress can prompt excessive tidiness or need to control.
- Pacing. This can be aggressive arousal and/or the sympathetic nervous system prompt to fight or flight.

- Puffing. This can signal a constant need to release pent-up tension.
- Eye-dart or stammering eye (fast blinking). Stress releases adrenalin which can cause accelerated blink-rate.
- Licking lips in a darting manner. A similarly produced response to eye-dart.
- Excessive swallowing. Adrenalin dries the throat and mouth.
- Jerky, dislocated movement. Stress creates dissonance between the sympathetic and parasympathetic nervous systems, meaning the desire to fight or flight is interspersed with a desire to sit still and relax. This inner conflict can cause dislocated movements.
- Nervous laughter or giggling. Not all laughter is prompted by fun. It can also be a nervous response.
- Shaking hands. Prompted by adrenalin.
- Wide eyes. We widen our eyes in response to shock or surprise. It's part of our survival system but inappropriate long-term. Doing it for long periods of time can signal fear or stress.

How to Spot Cut-Offs – They've Stopped Listening or Getting Involved

- Long blink. This can be a longer blink than usual or an eye-shut cut-off to make you go away.
- Looking down. A marginally more polite version of the above.
- Dropping head. Hiding the face in a childlike belief that when they look back up you'll have vanished!
- Turning completely away for a moment.
- Pushing chair back from desk or table. Creating distance might become important for them.

- Stacking paperwork and banging it on the table. A very obvious and annoying habit to signal a desire to end the meeting or conversation.
- Body barriers.
- Looking up towards the ceiling.

How to Spot Someone Is Listening with an Open Mind

- Increased eye contact. Especially if it increases while you speak. Normally in business you'd expect to see an initial performance of eye contact as part of the listening skills, but the gaze can diminish with time. If it starts to increase and you're not making them angry, prompting aggressive arousal, you could be capturing their attention.
- Nodding. Check the nod is in pace with your speech. If it's in tempo it's good news. If it's faster they want you to finish.
- Face-to-face torsos. This signals rapt or undivided attention.
- Mirroring you – you move first and they copy. This can be a good sign that they're locked into your ideas.
- Raised brows. Can signal interest and like, but not if it's done as a brief shrug, in which case it can mean disbelief.
- Smiling. Easy to spot? Not really. Stretched over-smiling can signal masked boredom or irritation. Look for asymmetric smiling that extends to (and might only include) the eyes.
- Leaning forward. This suggests they're engaged. Again beware, though. If they lean forward and stare they could be signalling very intense anger.
- Touching your arm or shoulder. Touch is good. Steering touch might be not so good, though. If they hold your

arm and start to push gently they could be trying to get you out of the office.

- Sitting leaning forward but without moving. This should signal intense listening.

How to Spot When Someone's Being Judgemental

- Mouth-shrug – often accompanied by a one-shoulder shrug. It involves pulling the corners of the mouth down and pushing the chin up slightly. If the chin is raised along with the head it's more likely to be an oxbow mouth, signalling defiance or stubbornness.
- Fingers covering mouth. Not the mouth-hide gesture of a liar but the more deliberate-looking placing of one finger (usually the index) vertically across the lips.
- Looking down at notes. They could be looking for proof of your claims.
- Palm-rocking. The hand is held out vertically and rocked backward and forward, signalling they're not impressed.
- Leg-lock. One leg is crossed across the other thigh. This is when the leg is raised so that the calf is placed across the thigh, forming a barrier.
- Leg-clamp. Ditto but with hands holding the top leg. This can increase the hint that they're not in agreement.
- Fingers to chin with index finger up the side of the face. Listening with an open mind can often entail putting the fingers to the chin but when the index finger is raised they're probably signalling you've still got a lot of work to do to convince them.
- Eye-narrowing. This is a classic signal of disbelief.
- Head tilts to one side and one eyebrow raises. The sideways head-tilt can signal listening but combined with the brow-raise it can mean disbelief.

- Both eyebrows raised with chin pulled in. You'd get this signal straight away. It looks rude and overly judgemental or sarcastic.
- Looking over the top of spectacles. I know there are several logical causes for this look but it can also be a signal of judgemental raised status.
- Steepling. A very precise gesture that can imply serious, high-status judgemental thought.

How to Spot Status-Boosting

- Pulling themselves up to full height to look bigger and make their head higher.
- Legs splayed. Splaying is a sign of alpha or physical status-boosting.
- Reading over your shoulder. This is intimidating. Although it might not be done for that purpose it should rightly prompt suspicions of Power Posturing.
- Standing too close. Spatial aggression can mean an attempt to intimidate.
- Invading your space or desk-space.
- Sitting or standing higher than you. Elevation is usually a sign they consider themselves higher in status or more powerful.

- Increased eye contact. This can be interest or intimidation.
- Hand or hands on hips. This is likely to be subconscious but body-bulking can signal Power Posturing.
- Strong-grip handshake. Crushing means domination.
- Patting you on the shoulder or back (if it's on the head I think you'll get the message anyway). The pat of power might look friendly but it's also a parental-style put-down. A clear sign they feel superior to you.
- Steepled fingers. To let you know they're being very precise and formal (see opposite).
- Puffed chest. Another alpha power gesture.
- Directing, dominant gestures like pointing and leading. The royals use what I call 'the pointless point' when they appear in public. This pointing at nothing in particular registers interest but it is also a group directional gesture of control.
- Raised chin. Again, raising the head means looking down on people, suggesting superiority.

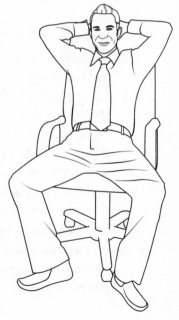

- Alpha behaviours, like sitting alone. Alpha apes tend to use space and solitude.
- Sitting using less movement than the rest of the group.
- Pit-baring, sitting with hands behind head. If they use this on you they're hinting you're no threat to them whatsoever.

- Instigating changes of posture or movement. In a group, especially a business group, the first person to instigate a change of body posture is usually the highest in status. The others will tend to follow suit.
- Sitting at the head of the board table. A classic power position.
- Using expansive but controlled gestures.

How to Spot if They're Wanting to Reach Agreement

- They mirror your body language. Like-bodied usually signals like-minded.
- Empathetic nodding, in time with your speech.
- Open gestures. While body-barriers or concealed hands will suggest hidden thoughts, open gestures that aren't over-performed will often mean agreement.
- Leaning forward. Body proximity is usually a sign of mental conformity
- Mirrored facial expressions. This is a very strong sign that they agree with your point.
- Palms turned out or upward. Done subtly this should suggest openness and welcome.
- Relaxed breathing patterns. Saying no or disagreeing can produce irregular breathing.
- Their torso is turned towards you.
- Feet pointed in your direction. Feet do tend to gesture desired direction. During difficult meetings I've seen many feet pointed towards the door!
- They perform speech pause signals when you speak, like placing a finger across their lips. This should mean they're keen to allow you to speak, which ought to mean interest. But only if the finger is bent or relaxed. If it's rigid they might be judgemental.

- They keep even eye contact when they're listening to you. This shouldn't be exaggerated or over-performed, though. Their eye expression should look relaxed.
- Their eyebrows are slightly raised. Slight arching is a sign of 'tell me more'.
- Their lips remain relaxed, not tightly closed or sucked in.
- If you're closing a sale, expect to see an increase of anxiety signals prior to agreement. This can include fiddling, edginess, nail-biting, rapid breathing, lip-licking, face-touching, etc. This can be misleading but it is a common part of the agreement process. Once the decision to buy has been made you will then see an explosion of relief signals, like laughing and smiling.

How to Spot if You're Wedged into Conflict or Anger

- Stuttering eye, an increased blink-rate. It's back to that adrenalin burst.
- Tightening of the lips. This is the muscle tension caused by aggressive arousal. If the top lip becomes as tight as a drum and is pulled back far enough to bare some of the top set of teeth, prepare for flight!
- Baring or jutting of lower jaw teeth. This is more of an aggressive pose, aimed to threaten rather than fight. It can be part of the fight build-up, though.
- Curling up of top lip. This is likely to be a performed signal of dislike or cynicism.
- A set look to the jaw. Muscle tension affects the jaw, even creating speech changes – that is, talking through clenched teeth.
- Hands curled into fists.
- Inability to keep still. Both pacing and constant movement can signal aggressive arousal as the body prepares for fight.

- Pointing. This involves the finger being used as a symbol of weaponry. For pointing (at you) read virtual stabbing. Watch their other gestures and cluster signals for confirmation.

- Aggressive gestures like chopping or dismissive hand-flapping.

- Arms folded high on the chest. This displays the arm muscles, protects the chest and makes the body look bulkier.

- Staring. If their eye contact increases to staring they're either in love with you or they want to attack. The difference is easy to spot. Love involves eye-softening. Anger makes the eyes bulge.

- Avoiding gaze altogether. This would come under the heading of ignoring, which can be aggressive. Make sure you're not seeing shyness, though. Aggressive ignoring usually involves a raised chin, as though they're too important to see you.

- Over-smiling, baring both sets of teeth. This displays teeth for the purpose of fight.

- Self-harm like scratching, pulling at own hair or hitting self. These could be displacement gestures, suggesting displaced aggression. The point is, who do they feel aggressive about?

Remember to be perceptive in the workplace, taking note of your colleagues' body language gestures but always keep in mind that no one gesture will ever 'give the game away'. Make sure you're firing on all cylinders, listening to what's said, watching for their general behaviour, looking for clues in things like the tone of their voice and monitoring their body language, both the 'performed' gestures and their 'leakage' signals.

Key Points:

- Never underestimate your killer occasions in the workplace. Plan, practise and rehearse.
- Remember, these are performance skills. Learn how to warm up and how to project. Merely 'being yourself' will not be enough!
- Get out of your comfort zone on a regular basis. The more you stretch yourself the better you will begin to feel.
- Remember, even small details like the way you hold your pen might leak more away about your inner feelings than you realised.
- Be visually aware. Although there are no exact symptoms when it comes to reading other people in the workplace, by increasing your eye-scanning you'll have a far greater understanding of the way their minds work.

SUMMARY

Although this book will have given you huge insights into how we think and behave, I do hope you won't become one of those body language know-alls who announce to all and sundry that they have almost mystical skills of mind-reading. Remember that there are no absolutes, but remember too that it's the very complexity of body language that makes it so fascinating. Your study of body language should be an on-going hobby or science. We're all experts and you probably began this book with much more knowledge than you realised.

Keep positive about your own skills. The greatest changes in your life will be achieved by sculpting your own body language to make it endorse what you say or to speak out on your behalf instead of heckling you. I've taken a tough tone because I know it's easy to give up once you begin to step outside your comfort zone, but I also know that the techniques I've shown you really do work.

The initial effort is worth it and, don't forget, no one's asking you to be perfect. Never try to clone yourself, but *do* bring all your best skills and personality traits to the surface. It's the differences that make us special, not the similarities.

BODY LANGUAGE DICTIONARY

A guide to terms, words and general jargon used either in this book or by other people!

Absorbed Actions: Those actions we pick up via subconscious copy.

Accelerated Blink-rate: When an adrenalin surge, caused by stress or anger, makes the blink-rate increase.

Active-listening Signals: Actions that include nodding, facial mirroring, tilting the head, etc., to show you're listening to someone.

Adaptors: The name given to the small gestures someone makes when in a state of cognitive dissonance or anxiety. This would include self-comfort gestures such as facial touch.

Aggressive Arousal: A state of anger where physical symptoms are produced. In body language terms this can be jaw-tightening, muscle-clenching and the use of fists or ritualised weapons like finger-pointing or head-batoning.

Air-hump: The subtle pelvic jerks that a man may do while talking to his friends when he sees a woman he fancies.

Air-kiss: A cheek-to-cheek kiss that may not involve touching.

Alerting Signals: Raising a hand, removing spectacles, doing eye-flashes (see page 128), etc., to show a desire to speak.

Ambivalent Signals: Using different signals, both of which are genuine, performed at the same time but send out different messages.

Ankle-lock Gesture: Standing with your ankles crossed together.

Announcement Gesture: Aka alerting signal.

Asymmetric Smiling: A crooked smile.

Auto-contact Gestures: Self-touch.

Autonomic Signals: Stress-promoted actions or body changes, like fidgeting, fast breathing, accelerated blink-rate, pallor or flushing, crying, etc.

Back-channel Signals: Gestures that encourage a speaker, like nodding.

Barrier Gestures: The hands, arms or legs will attempt to 'protect' their owner from 'attack', or props can be used to the same effect. Barrier gestures could be folded arms and legs, a raised wine glass or a handbag pulled across the chest. Certain types of fiddling, like playing with a cuff or moving the strap of a handbag, can also be performed to created a temporary barrier pose.

Baton Signals: Any gesture that emphasises the pace of the words.

Beachball Hands: A term coined during the last election when Michael Howard tended to talk with both hands raised as though clutching and rotating an imaginary beachball. Since copied by many other speakers when displaying the size of a problem.

Body Contact Tie-signs: The way close friends or lovers touch each other to communicate in public.

Body-guide: Using small movements like pats or touches to steer someone.

Celebratory Displays: These can be instinctive, resulting from an adrenalin burst caused by a win, including leaps in the air, running, air-punching or dancing; restrained, as in a modest smile or small air-punch; or even performed in place of a win. Losing contestants or award nominees will often smile and throw their arms in the air when they hear that someone else has won.

Closure Signals: The way we signal a conversation is over, e.g. cutting down the back-channel signals, looking around the room, etc.

Cluster Signals: An overall view of someone's body language gestures.

Cognitive Algebra: The way the mind pieces together various stimuli and signals, often visual, to produce an overall impression of the subject.

Cognitive Dissonance: This can occur when the brain is sent conflicting messages or signals, as in incongruent communications.

Comfort Gestures: These can be symbolic, like a speaker opening his or her arms towards the audience in an empty embrace, or more personal, like a touch or hug.

Complementary Body Language: This occurs when two or more speakers talk from the same body language state, or a state that is sought by the other speaker. For instance two friends chatting might both use animated gestures and smiles. However it would also be complementary if one person was dominant and dictatorial and the other submissive and compliant.

Compound Gestures: Gestures that require several stages or disciplines of movement.

Congruent Signals: This occurs when the visual, verbal and vocal communications all send out the same message, making the speaker appear honest and convincing.

Contradictory Signals: When two contradictory signals are sent out, usually where one is honest and one a lie.

Crotch-over Gestures: Also known as fig-leaf displays, usually a male gesture of insecurity.

Crotch-displays: Any subconscious or overt attempt to get attention in the crotch area, e.g. sitting with legs splayed, etc.

Cues: Body language cues refers to the way we draw conclusions about someone from looking at them.

Cut-off Signals: Usually a dropping of the head or closing of the eyes to register lack of interest or attention or a desire to be somewhere else.

Dead-fish: A limp handshake.

Delayed Gratification: Someone who pauses before or delays moments of pleasure, usually to enjoy or relish the anticipation or enhance the pleasure.

Denial Gestures: These are often small body language gestures and/or expressions that appear to disagree with or scupper the speaker's key point. They are generally prompted by embarrassment or a desire to be liked and will usually appear at the end of a talk or presentation. They usually take the form of eye-rolls, mouth- or shoulder-shrugs or even silly walks back to your seat.

Discovered Actions: Gestures or movements we acquire without thinking about it, often because of comfort, e.g. folding the arms.

Displacement Signals: When you carry out the body language ritual or movement on someone or something other than the person that prompted the emotion, e.g. biting your own lip when you get angry with someone else.

Distance Displays: Greeting or acknowledgement gestures used from a distance, e.g. waving, etc.

Distracted Kiss: This occurs when two people come together to kiss but one or both looks over the other's shoulder as the kiss occurs. This is usually seen as insulting as the distracted kisser appears to be looking around for something or someone more interesting.

Distraction Signals: Seen in apes and humans at moments of agitation. These appear counter-productive, e.g. yawning during times of great fear or stopping to groom, etc.

Dog-facing: A deadpan, downtrodden expression, often used when there are figures of authority present.

Emotional Intelligence: Having the ability to be empathetic and 'see' what other people are feeling or 'read' other people.

Emphatic Gestures: These are quite exaggerated hand, head or even foot gestures that endorse the verbal message by accentuating its sentiments.

Empty Embrace: When a speaker holds his or her arms out towards the audience in a gesture that mimics an invitation to embrace.

Erect Thumb: This is primarily a male signal of enjoyment, also known as a 'thumbs up'. The thumb goes up and even back, like a gun that's been cocked. It can occur during consumption of food, the playing of sport or even during a confident or winning moment at work.

Expressions: Facial movements, facial expressions.

Extended Gaze: When the eye contact lingers it is usually a sign of love, lust or anger.

Eye-block Gesture: When a listener performs long, slow blinks, ostensibly to blank you out when they become bored.

Eye Contact: When a speaker and/or listener looks into the eyes of the other person.

Eye-flash: A sudden intense and meaningful glance, often for warning or to obtain agreement.

Eye-gaze: Usually prolonged in lovers, creating the concept 'love at first sight'. Normal eye-gaze can be an intentional gesture though, signalling where the gazer would really like to be, e.g the exit.

Eye-puff: Widening the eyes by pulling the lids back.

Eye-shrug: When the eyes are raised temporarily heavenward, usually in a gesture of exasperation.

Eye-shuffle: Looking quickly from side to side in an attempt to find escape.

Eye-stutter: Irregular blinking, signalling confusion.

Face-framing: Holding your hands around your face during a conversation in an attempt to make the other person focus on that area of your body.

Finger-baton: When the finger (usually the index finger) is held erect and waggled at someone, implying a desire to hit or beat them into submission.

Finger-counting: A way of holding an audience's attention or letting them know you want to say more, counting your points off on your fingers while holding them at chest level.

Gated Hands: Made famous by Tony Blair, the gated hands is a term I coined to describe his habit of constantly holding both hands in front of his chest with palms turned inward, like a gate that he then kept opening out and closing tight. A gesture that suggests closed thoughts or dominant status.

Gestures: Actions that send out signals. Usually performed with the hands.

Grooming Display: This can be real, as in picking a hair from someone's jacket or self-grooming, e.g. touching your own hair, or it can be ritualised, the body language equivalent of small talk.

Hamster Hands: A term I coined to describe a habit women have of talking with their hands clasped high on their chest, like a hamster clutching a sunflower seed.

Hand Chop: A gesture of anger or signalling the end of a discussion or conversation. The hand is literally used like a chopper, sometimes landing on a desk or the other palm.

Hand-sandwich: A two-handed handshake, also referred to as the Glove.

Hand-swat: Displaying the back of the hand towards someone and then miming swatting or pushing them away with it.

Head-baton: Popular with impassioned speakers like Neil Kinnock, the head-baton involves swiping the head or pushing it through the air to illustrate commitment.

Hug-patting: When a couple hug, the pat is a recognised sign to break. Men tend to over-pat during man-on-man hugs to signal there's no sexual motive.

Illustrative Gestures: The hands are used to mime or define what the person is talking about.

Inborn Actions: Gestures you do by instinct, rather than learn or copy.

Incongruent Body Language: When the words, tone or body language signals appear to be out of tune – i.e. saying different things. In this case it is usually the body language that is seen as the most credible.

Inconvenience Displays: The more a host inconveniences him- or herself to greet a visitor the greater the apparent status of the visitor, e.g. standing to greet someone or even waiting out on the street when their car arrives.

Instant Gratification: Someone taking what they want when they want it, rather than waiting.

Intentional Eye-gaze: The eyes look towards the true area of interest or the place the gazer would like to be or intends to be.

Intentional Gesture: Any gesture that gives warning of the gesture or movement that is to follow.

Interactional Synchronisation: When people move in the same way. This seems like coincidence but can often be a result of following each other's body language cues.

Intimate Territory: The zone of space around us that we are only comfortable with close friends or family members invading.

Jaw-jut: Sticking out the lower jaw, usually to display displeasure or the sulk state. It can also be an aggressive signal. When the jaw is jutted towards an enemy it can be a strong sign of defiance.

Killer Walk: A term coined by me for my book *Sex Signals*, where I explained how vital a smooth, sensual walking style can be as part of the attraction process.

Leading: This is where someone will mirror another person's body language before changing their own state in a bid to lead the other person to do the same.

Leakage: This occurs when your body language 'leaks' out your true feelings in one or a series of give-away gestures.

Leg-clamp: This usually follows the leg lock, when the hands grip on to the upper leg.

Leg-lock Gesture: When the legs are crossed but with the upper leg crossed high, across the thigh of the lower leg.

Lightning Smile: As used by Gordon Brown, the lightning smile disappears just as quickly as it appears, like a bolt of lightning coming out of the blue.

Lowered Steeple: When the fingers are steepled with the tips pointing towards the ground, usually a sign of critical listening.

Masking: Performing body language expressions or gestures to deliberately mask your true feelings. This can be done for deliberate deception or to be socially polite.

Matador Stab: Term coined by me during the 2005 election to describe the over-emphatic method of nailing a point by pointing both index fingers towards the lectern and stabbing them in a downwards direction. Used frequently by both Tony Blair and Gordon Brown.

Metronomic Gestures: A term I coined to describe finger, foot or even pen-drumming/tapping. This works like a mini-metronome, placing pressure on a speaker to hurry up.

Micro-gestures: Fleeting gestures or facial movements that can be almost invisible to the naked eye, but which are nonetheless seen as significant in body language terms. Often analysed by watching video footage in slow motion.

Mime Gestures: As the name implies, these gestures tend to mime the action they describe, like wobbling a hand in front of the face when asking if someone would like a drink, or placing the thumb by the ear and the little finger to the mouth to signal 'call me'.

Mimic Gestures: Gestures that mime or copy real objects or actions.

Mirroring: This is a term for postural echo, although mirroring will usually be applied to conscious copying of another person's movements or pace to create a feeling of empathy or rapport.

Mirthless Smile: Term coined by me to describe wide mouth-smiles that don't reach the eyes.

Mock-attack Gestures: Ritualised attack movements that can be used as a first-stage sexual exploration/flirt ritual or just to break down formality.

Mouth-shrugs: The mouth-shrug resembles a small, upturned smile with the chin crumpled, the lips raised in the middle and dropped at the corners. It's a very common social 'smile', especially in the workplace. It suggests long-suffering and stoicism.

Non-verbal Leakage: Body language give-aways.

Overcongruent Body Language: When the speaker overexaggerates his or her gestures or facial expressions to put the message across. This overacting is often seen as false or patronising.

Overkill Signals: Over-reaction signals.

Oxbow Mouth: Similar to the mouth-shrug but with a firmer chin and jaw line, signalling determination or even stubbornness.

Pacing: Picking up on someone's pace of movement and copying it to create empathy.

Palm Displays: Showing the palm can be considered a signal of honesty unless it's over-displayed.

Palm-rocking: Waving a hand from side to side to signal 'maybe'.

Personal Heckling: When your body language signals appear to disagree with your verbal message.

Personal Zone: A distance of about 45–100cm around someone.

Physiological Signals: Physical body language responses like blushing, sweating, etc.

Pinging Smile: A sudden, exaggerated smile.

Pit-baring: A term I coined to describe the act of sitting back and placing your hands behind your head. This bares all the delicate body parts, including the armpits, and suggests arrogance. Women might toss their hair around or preen to get the same effect.

Pointless Point: A term I coined to describe the way royals and some politicians point towards nothing in particular in public to feign interest and act directive and in charge.

Poker Face: Used by poker players to avoid other players reading their expression, this method of sitting very still and moving very little, with a deadpan facial expression, is often used outside the poker room.

Postural Congruence: Sitting or standing in the same way as others.

Postural Echo: Like mirroring, copying someone's body language and pace of movement, possibly without realising.

Power-pat: Power-patting is another status-boosting gesture used by politicians and the like. The shoulder-pat is a signal of almost parental approval. Therefore, by patting another politician or world statesman at a critical moment the patter manages to appear friendly but at the same time takes the parental and therefore higher-status role.

Power-shake: Handshakes that are intended to emphasise high power or status, like getting your hand on top in the shake or crushing the other person's hand.

Precision Gesture: Often a pinching together of the thumb and index finger with the fingers pointing upward to suggest precise, exact knowledge.

Primary Emotions: Your instinctive emotions like fear, anger, etc.

Pseudo-infantile Re-motivator: Displays of childish helplessness used to promote non-critical, nurturing responses.

Public Zone: Distance of over 12 feet from another.

Pupil Dilation: Usually occurs when the watcher looks at something pleasant or someone they love. Courtesans in earlier centuries used to put drops of belladonna, a poison, in their eyes to mimic the effect.

Raised Steeple: When a steepling gesture is performed with all the fingers pointing upward.

Relic Gestures: Any gesture that has outlived its original meaning.

Re-motivating Action: An action or gesture used to close down the existing mood and replace it with a new one. Apes that feel threatened will often employ flirt signals to change the aggressive ape's thoughts from fight to sex.

Rictus: A rigid, stretched smile.

Ritualised Combat: Gestures that mimic aggressive or fight gestures, used as a warning albeit subconsciously, e.g. pacing, making fists, jutting the jaw, etc.

Salutation Displays: Forms of greeting.

Schematic Gestures: More stylised or abbreviated versions of mimic gestures.

Scissors Stance: Standing with your legs crossed.

Screensaver Face: A term I coined to describe the face we pull in between social displays, usually a deadpan, or even angry or anxious-looking face.

Scrotch: The scratching or hoiking of the crotch area to gain sexual attention, usually performed by males.

Secondary Emotions: Emotions that are prompted by your own thoughts, like worry or anxiety.

Self-motivational Gestures: These are a little like winding up a clock – i.e. turning one hand around in a circle, pacing back and forth, etc. – in a bid to get the brain into top gear.

Self-policing: When someone is so aware of their body language they begin to self-correct visibly.

Self-reward Gestures: Jumping in the air, hugging yourself, etc.

Self-stab Gesture: Poking your own finger or pen into yourself.

Self-stroke: Stroking any part of your body, usually to either self-calm or to seduce.

Shortfall Signals: Under-reaction signals.

Signature Gestures: Any gesture frequently or possibly famously used by someone, especially a celebrity.

Social Zone: Distance of 5–10 feet away from another person.

Spatial Behaviour: Your use of space in relation to others.

Spatial Rituals: The way people tend to keep patterns of space in certain situations.

Splaying: Standing or sitting with legs wide apart.

Status Displays: How we show our real or ideal status to the world at large.

Steepling Gestures: Any hand gesture where the fingers are linked or pointed upwards in the shape of a steeple. Usually seen as a Power Posture.

Stotting: Taken from the animal kingdom, a bouncing style of walk used to signal energy and enthusiasm in order to attract a mate.

Stretched Social Smile: The wide, over-exaggerated smiling that people do at boring social events.

Submissive Signals: Status-lowering or compliant signals like body-lowering or gaze-dropping.

Suppressed Smile: When the lips are pressed together to minimise or conceal a smile.

Symbolic Gestures: Used to signal feelings or ideas.

Sympathetic Nervous System: Prompts fight/flight responses while parasympathetic system attempts to self-calm.

Technical Gestures: Trained gestures used in certain professions where speech might not be possible.

Tell: The terms 'tell' and 'show' have been coined by some psychologists to describe body language signals.

Territorial Behaviour: Body language marking of territory or ownership.

Thumb of Power: Usually referring to pointing with the knuckles but also placing the thumb down on top of the knuckles in a power gesture. Used a lot by politicians.

Tie-signs: Silent, subtle body language signals that people in a close relationship throw to one another, like a nod, pat or eye-roll, etc.

Tongue-flick: A very quick tongue-dart, often caused by embarrassment.

Tongue-lick: When the tongue licks around the lips and corners of the mouth, signalling pleasure or anticipation, possibly sexual.

Tongue-poke: When the tongue is displayed at the middle of the mouth, signalling rejection or disgust.

Trained Actions: Gestures and movements we have to learn, like typing or changing gear in a car.

Transfix: Holding a pose when you've been interrupted while speaking to show a desire to return to your point.

Triumph Displays: Raised arms, air-punching, etc. Any performed or spontaneous gesture that raises the status at a point of victory or pseudo-victory.

Truncated Gestures: Any unfinished gesture.

Weighing Hands: A two-handed gesture when hands seem to mimic weighing scales, signalling the speaker is weighing up options.

Wrapping: Wrapping yourself in your hands or arms, like self-hugging. A self-comfort gesture.

Zones of Proximity: How close you stand to someone else. (Usually defined as three key zones. See *Personal Zone*, *Public Zone* and *Social Zone*.)

INDEX

INDEX

INDEX

INDEX